THE BOOK
of
WORDS

AN ENTERTAINING LOOK AT WORDS AND HOW WE HAVE COME TO USE THEM

TIM GLYNNE-JONES

ARCTURUS

ARCTURUS

This edition published in 2008 by Arcturus Publishing Limited
26/27 Bickels Yard, 151–153 Bermondsey Street,
London SE1 3HA

ISBN: 978-1-84193-948-3

Printed in China

CONTENTS

INTRODUCTION

There are almost 7,000 languages being used in the world today, yet somehow English has emerged as the predominant one. This is mainly due to political history, but it is also due in no small part to the words themselves, of which there are estimated to be a greater number than in any other language on Earth.

This vast resource of words has fed the creative genius of the world's most famous wordsmiths, from Shakespeare to The Beatles, as well as enabling its everyday users to speak in varied and colourful ways, to adapt quickly and easily to the changing needs of science and technology, to play games, to impress one another with big, complicated words or to communicate just about anywhere in the world with short, simple ones.

This is not a dictionary or a grammar book, though there are definitions and rules throughout. Its real purpose is to take a snapshot of the English language as it stands in these early years of the 21st century, so readers can reflect on the words we use, where they come from, how they develop, how we put them together, who makes the rules and why words inspire such a range of emotions.

There is a word in English for every possible need, and when a new need arises, we quickly invent a new one. This ability to evolve is what makes English the predominant global language today.

Enjoy it while it lasts!

A

'A Norse, a Norse, my kingdom for a Norse.'

The first letter of most European alphabets, 'a' has a multitude of uses in English. It is mostly employed as a prefix but there are two very common instances in which 'a' stands alone as a proper, upstanding word.

The first is when it is used as the indefinite article: *a* cat, *a* dog, *a* word.

In this instance it is derived from 'an' – the other indefinite article, originally meaning 'one' – which was used exclusively in Old English until the 12th century, when the 'n' started to be left out when it was placed before a consonant.

> 'WE'VE BOUGHT AN DOG.'
> 'HAVE YOU? THAT'S AN DAFT THING TO DO.'

Today both 'a' and 'an' can still be used to mean specifically 'one', as in 'It weighs an ounce' or 'You owe me a pound'.

Some people still insist on keeping the 'n' before words beginning with soft consonants;: for example, *an* hotel. But opinion is divided. Merriam-Webster's *Dictionary of English Usage* says you should use the article that suits your pronunciation. So if you prefer to say 'an 'otel', that's up to you.

Many words in modern English were formed by this conjunction of the indefinite article and the old noun. A good example is 'nickname'. This term evolved from the Old English 'eke-name', 'eke' meaning extra*, but 'an eke-name' became 'a neke-name' and then 'a nick-name'. Similarly, 'an apron' used to be 'a napron', and you can see the connection with 'napkin', a napron being a small tablecloth.

---

* *These days eke is either used in the sense of working hard for a small return, as in 'eke out a living', or making things go further. You might eke out a meal to feed an unexpected guest, which comes from the original meaning – to make things go a bit further.*

The second instance in which 'a' appears extensively as a word in its own right is as an alternative to the Latin 'per', as in 'miles a minute', 'pence a litre', etc. This too is an abbreviation of the Old English 'an', which also meant 'on', or 'on each' in this case. 'A' could perhaps also be seen as a word in its own right when English takes on the French 'à', meaning 'at', 'on' or 'to', in numerous adopted phrases, such as 'tête à tête', 'à la carte', etc.

When 'a' is used as a prefix, the previous derivation of 'on' also leads to the use of 'a' in making adjectives from nouns.

❖ ABOARD ❖ AFLOAT ❖ ASHORE

In earlier times 'a' was also used to mean 'to' or 'at', as seen in 19th century novels: 'I am going abed'.

Finally, 'a' can mean 'not' – as in 'asexual' or 'amoral', for instance. This sense derives from the Greek 'a' or 'an', or in some cases the Latin 'ab', still used in modern English; for example, 'abnormal'.

See also THE.

AARDVARK

A mysterious and little understood animal, the aardvark is nevertheless familiar throughout the world, thanks to that typographical attribute the double 'a'. Popular amongst businesses looking to appear first in alphabetical listings, a Google search for aardvark returns 4.55 million results, compared to 1.3 million for tapir and just 407,000 for dromedary.

The first ten of these include a travel company, a recruitment agency, a record company, a design studio and a website for rude jokes. The point being that most mentions of aardvark have nothing to do with the animal itself – a nocturnal mammal native to sub-Saharan Africa, which feeds on ants and termites. Also known as the antbear, its name comes from the Afrikaans '*aarde varken*', meaning earth pig.

ABBREVIATION

The evolution of language sees an increasing tendency towards the abbreviation (shortening) of words or phrases. Abbreviations occur in all fields, from youth culture to sport to technology, but only a relative handful become commonly used words in their own right. Probably the most commonly used abbreviation in the English language is 'pub', short for 'public house'. Here are some other common examples:

ADMIN	⇨ *administration*
ANON	⇨ *anonymous*
APPROX	⇨ *approximately*
BROS	⇨ *brothers*
CO	⇨ *company*
DIS	⇨ *disrespect*
DIV	⇨ *division*
DOC	⇨ *document*
ESQ	⇨ *esquire*
FAN	⇨ *fanatic*
FAX	⇨ *facsimile*
FIG	⇨ *figure*
HI-FI	⇨ *high fidelity*
INC	⇨ *incorporated*
MESSRS	⇨ *Messieurs (French for misters)*
MR	⇨ *Mister*
MRS	⇨ *Missus*
OBIT	⇨ *obituary*
PECS	⇨ *pectoral muscles*
PEN	⇨ *penalty/penitentiary (US)*

PUB	⇨ *public house*
REPS	⇨ *repetitions/representatives*
SECS	⇨ *seconds*
SUB	⇨ *substitute*
TEL	⇨ *telephone*
XMAS	⇨ *Christmas*

See also ACRONYM; TEXTING LANGUAGE; XMAS.

An acronym is a word formed from the initial letters of the words in a phrase or title. In most cases these are obvious abbreviations of the names of companies or organizations: for example, NATO (North Atlantic Treaty Organization) and NASA (National Aeronautics and Space Administration), but some examples have gone on to become everyday words and expressions.

◆**AIDS** ⋗ *Acquired Immune Deficiency Syndrome* ◆**AWOL** ⋗ *Absent Without Leave* ◆**BOGOF** ⋗ *Buy One Get One Free* ◆**LASER** ⋗ *Light Amplification by Stimulated Emission of Radiation* ◆**RADAR** ⋗ *Radio Detecting and Ranging* ◆**RAM** ⋗ *Random Access Memory* ◆**ROM** ⋗ *Read-only memory* ◆**SCUBA** ⋗ *Self-Contained Underwater Breathing Apparatus* ◆**WAP** ⋗ *Wireless Application Protocol* ◆**WYSIWYG** ⋗ *What You See Is What You Get*

Another well-known acronym is QWERTY, which, as any typist will tell you, is the name of the standard typewriter or computer keyboard, derived from the letters in the first six positions in the top row of letters (see Typewriter). Such is our love of acronyms that unusual words are often assumed to be acronyms, or are made into acronyms via a reverse process ('bacronyms'). The most famous example is the word 'posh', which is commonly believed to stand for 'Port Out, Starboard Home'. The explanation runs that the most expensive cabins on ships sailing to the East would be situated on the port side on the outward journey and the starboard side on the return journey, because that way they were shielded from the sun.

See also MNEMONIC.

ADJECTIVE

An adjective is a word that modifies a noun; in other words, it tells you something about that noun. However, not all words that modify nouns are adjectives. But let's concentrate on those that are first.

Adjectives can often be recognized by their endings.

ABLE ❖	*likeable, breakable, drinkable*	IC ❖	*acidic, climatic, metric*
ANT ❖	*ignorant, expectant, jubilant*	ISH ❖	*childish, impish, mawkish*
ENT ❖	*cognoscent, innocent, decadent*	IVE ❖	*attractive, festive, furtive*
FUL ❖	*helpful, beautiful, artful*	LESS ❖	*hopeless, shameless, faultless*
IBLE ❖	*incredible, convertible, risible*	LIKE ❖	*childlike, apelike, lifelike*
		OUS ❖	*joyous, copious, jealous*
		Y ❖	*fluffy, cloudy, smarmy*

But, typical of the English language, there are many adjectives that do not have a regular, recognizable form.

big ♦♦♦ small	old ♦♦♦ young	clever ♦♦♦ stupid
light ♦♦♦ dark	wide ♦♦♦ narrow	good ♦♦♦ bad

In most cases you'll find that these words are of Germanic origin, having come into English with the Northern European invaders, the Angles, Saxons, Jutes and Vikings. The adjectives with obvious endings were formed later, either from Greek or Latin roots – for example 'ignorant' – or by combining Anglo-

Saxon words – for example 'childlike'.

Another rule that applies to most, but not all, adjectives is that they themselves can be modified, either comparatively – for example bigger – or superlatively – for example biggest. With many adjectives this is a simple process of adding 'er' or 'est' to the root word.

> *big* ➣ *bigger* ➣ *biggest*
> *small* ➣ *smaller* ➣ *smallest*
> *clever* ➣ *cleverer* ➣ *cleverest*
> *wide* ➣ *wider* ➣ *widest*

However, there are plenty of adjectives that buck this rule too.

> *bad* ➣ *worse* ➣ *worst*
> *good* ➣ *better* ➣ *best*

And others, usually the polysyllabic adjectives derived from Latin, rather than the monosyllabic ones derived from Anglo-Saxon, require the use of 'more' and 'most' (or 'less' and 'least'). This applies to those with regular endings, as per the first list, with the exception of adjectives ending in 'y', whereby the 'y' changes to an 'i' and the normal comparative and superlative endings are applied.

> attractive ◆ more attractive ◆ most attractive
> helpful ◆ more helpful ◆ most helpful
> ignorant ◆ more ignorant ◆ most ignorant
> joyous ◆ more joyous ◆ most joyous
> likeable ◆ more likeable ◆ most likeable
> cloudy ◆ cloudier ◆ cloudiest

NB: A common transgression of grammatical rules, although not one to lose sleep over, is the use of the superlative when distinguishing between two things. For example, many people might say 'Which of the twins is the best at running?'

However, when comparing two things the accepted rule is to use the comparative: 'Between apples and pears I like pears better.' Superlatives are used when comparing more than two things: 'Of all the fruit in the world, I like pears best.'

Absolutely perfect

Adjectives that cannot be modified are called absolute adjectives. There are no degrees of meaning involved with these modifiers. For example:

infinite ✦ main ✦ only ✦ parallel ✦ perfect ✦ unique

Sometimes an adjective replaces the noun it describes altogether, for example 'The meek shall inherit the Earth'. In this case 'The meek' is used in place of 'The meek people'. This is called a substantive adjective.

So when is a noun modifier not an adjective? Think about a football pitch. 'Football' tells us more about the pitch but the pitch cannot be described as 'football'. This is a noun doing the work of an adjective.

Sometimes a phrase will modify a noun as in, for example, 'a cause worth dying for', where 'worth dying for' modifies the noun 'cause'.

ADVERB

An adverb describes a verb, an adjective or another adverb. Adverbs answer the questions 'how?', 'when?', 'where?' and 'how much?'

HOW	**?**	quickly, passionately, loudly
WHEN	**?**	often, seldom, never
WHERE	**?**	everywhere, upwards, beside
HOW MUCH	**?**	very, as, least

Most adverbs are easily identified by their 'ly' ending, though not all words taking 'ly' endings are exclusively adverbs. For example, lovely, slovenly, timely and friendly are words in which the 'ly' suffix, derived from the Germanic *lik* and now evident in the German suffix *lich* (*plötzlich* = suddenly), is added to nouns rather than adjectives.

Another common ending is 'wise', as in clockwise, or, to a lesser extent, 'ways', as in sideways. Both suffixes have the same origin, 'wise' having largely replaced 'ways' over the years.

As with adjectives, adverbs can be modified into comparative and superlative forms by using 'as', 'more', 'less', 'most' and 'least'.

quickly ◆ as quickly ◆ more quickly ◆ most quickly

In a sentence such as this – 'The dark green car drove into the newly built garage.' – both 'dark' and 'newly' are adverbs, 'dark' modifying the adjective 'green' and 'newly' modifying 'built'.

Some words serve alone as both adverbs and adjectives; for example, 'late'.

The train was late – 'late' as an adjective modifying the noun 'train'.

The train was running late – 'late' as an adverb modifying the verb 'running'.

See also SUFFIX.

ALLITERATION

'If Peter Piper picked a peck of pickled pepper
Where's the peck of pickled pepper Peter Piper picked?'

This famous tongue-twister is a shining example of alliteration, which is defined as the repetition of the leading letter or sound in a succession of words – not to be confused with assonance.

The word comes from the Latin *littera*, meaning letter, with the prefix 'ad', meaning to, in the sense of adherence to or promotion of. The same root gives us 'obliterate', which generally means to wipe out of existence, but literally derives from a sense of rubbing out, removing from record.

See also ASSONANCE.

ALPHABET

The alphabet that contains the 26 letters that make up all English words was formalized in the 17th century, when the vowels 'i' and 'u' were made distinct from 'j' and 'v', of which they had been a variant up to that point.

The letters of the alphabet were adopted in Western Europe from Latin, which in turn took its alphabet from the Greeks. The same is true of the word 'alphabet' itself, which is derived from the first two letters of the Greek alphabet, alpha and beta.

In 1930, Heinz introduced Alphabetti Spaghetti, a variant of Heinz Spaghetti, comprising pasta shaped into letters of the alphabet, covered in tomato sauce and packaged in a tin. For 60 years it provided an amusing distraction for children, who could form rude words on the side of their plates during dinner, before being canned (pardon the pun) in 1990. But, much to the delight of teatime linguists, Alphabetti Spaghetti was reintroduced by Heinz in 2005.

During World War One, British signallers invented a phonetic alphabet that used words to represent letters so they could transmit their messages more clearly. The term 'ack-ack', for example, was used instead of 'AA' for anti-aircraft. This idea evolved into various alternative forms of phonetic alphabet, which were fine-tuned until 1956, when the version (right) commonly known as the NATO Phonetic Alphabet was drawn up for shipping, aviation and the military. This is not to be confused with the International Phonetic Alphabet, which is used to denote the precise pronunciation of letters and words.

ALPHA
BRAVO
CHARLIE
DELTA
ECHO
FOXTROT
GOLF
HOTEL
INDIA
JULIET
KILO
LIMA
MIKE
NOVEMBER
OSCAR
PAPA
QUEBEC
ROMEO
SIERRA
TANGO
UNIFORM
VICTOR
WHISKY
XRAY
YANKEE
ZULU

See also MORSE CODE; PHONETICS.

AMERICANISM

Ask any American what language they speak and in most cases they will tell you it's English. However, American English has developed a vocabulary all of its own. Some words have taken the notion of independence literally: even with the proliferation of Americanisms constantly entering the English language they have yet to establish themselves on this side of the pond.

English	American	English	American
◎ bill	✪ check	◎ pavement	✪ sidewalk
◎ bonnet	✪ hood	◎ petrol	✪ gas
◎ boot	✪ trunk	◎ rubber	✪ eraser
◎ braces	✪ suspenders	◎ semi-detached	✪ duplex
◎ bum	✪ fanny	◎ skip	✪ dumpster
◎ dummy	✪ pacifier	◎ stretcher	✪ gurney
◎ estate agent	✪ realtor	◎ tournament	✪ tourney
◎ ice lolly	✪ popsicle	◎ trainers	✪ sneakers
◎ ketchup	✪ catsup	◎ trousers	✪ pants
◎ lavatory	✪ bathroom		

Why these words have failed to permeate English English is anyone's guess, when plenty of other Americanisms have been enthusiastically adopted in Britain and beyond.

APARTMENT ☆ BALL PARK ☆ BUDDY ☆ CAB ☆ COOKIE ☆ COP ☆ DUDE ☆
ELEVATOR ☆ FRIES ☆ GARBAGE ☆ GUY ☆ PARKING LOT ☆ TRUCK ☆ VACATION

It's not only new words or phrases that divide English English and American English, it's also the way words are used. Take 'good', for example. Ask somebody in Britain how they are and they'll usually say, 'I'm well.' Ask an American and they'll say, 'I'm good.' As with so many Americanisms, this use of 'good' has been adopted in Britain amongst speakers who regard American English as cool, but is the source of constant annoyance amongst those who don't. For them, 'good' means 'of quality or merit' or 'virtuous'; children are good when they do what they're told. Happily, American English has also fed back with some very useful expressions about which there can be no complaints.

BEDROCK ☆ BOTTOM DOLLAR ☆ GERRYMANDER ☆ GRIDLOCK ☆ HATCHBACK ☆
LAME DUCK ☆ LEFT FIELD ☆ PASS THE BUCK ☆ RAINCHECK ☆ RAW DEAL ☆ STAKE
A CLAIM ☆ SUPERMARKET ☆ TAILGATE ☆ WHITE/BLUE COLLAR WORKER

At the same time, American English has disposed of certain words more commonly used in Britain; the word 'and', for example, the fourth most commonly used word in the English language, as in 'Let's go eat.'

But many words that have become obsolete in Britain have been preserved in America: fall (autumn), faucet (tap), diaper (nappy) and skillet (frying-pan) were all originated in Britain.

For all the simplified spellings (centre to center, colour to color, etc.), in many ways American English is

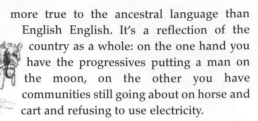

more true to the ancestral language than English English. It's a reflection of the country as a whole: on the one hand you have the progressives putting a man on the moon, on the other you have communities still going about on horse and cart and refusing to use electricity.

It's worth pointing out at this point that the suffix 'ize', so often branded an Americanization of the English 'ise', is actually not an Americanization at all. The United States declared independence in 1776; 'realize' was being written with a 'z' in England in 1611. It derives from the Greek suffix *izein* (*izare* in Latin), which was used to form verbs. It was the French who changed the 'z' to an 's', and this then influenced English. So there's nothing un English about the suffix 'ize', other, that is, than instances where the verb is not formed from the Greek suffix. Exercise, for example, should not be spelt with a 'z'. You can check in most cases by seeing if there is a related noun ending in '-ism'. For example, commercial gives the noun commercialism and the verb commercialize. Analysis (not analism) should give 'analyse' rather than 'analize', although analyze is acceptable.

America stands accused of corrupting the English language through the liberal use of suffixes like 'ize' and prefixes like 'dis' to create big new words such as disincentivize. But it was a practice that became almost an obsession in England during the 17th century, so when George W. Bush said, 'They misunderestimated me,' he was only trying to conform to a trend set in the 'old country' 500 years ago.

Bush, however, does seem to have discovered a form of English that nobody else is aware of. Maybe they teach it at Yale. See if you can misundecodify it:

'*I want you to know that farmers are not going to be secondary thoughts to a Bush administration. They will be in the forethought of our thinking.*'

✳

'*Will the highways on the Internet become more few?*'

✳

'*I've heard he's been called Bush's poodle. He's bigger than that.*'

✳

'*This process has been drug out a long time, which says to me it's political.*'

✳

'*And my concern, David, is several.*'

✳

'*I think that the vice president is a person reflecting a half-glass-full mentality.*'

✳

'*I want to thank you for the importance that you've shown for education and literacy.*'

✳

'*I can only speak to myself.*'

'*Families is where our nation finds hope, where wings take dream.*'

✳

'*I know the human being and fish can coexist peacefully.*'

✳

'*I think if you say you're going to do something and don't do it, that's trustworthiness.*'

✳

'*We cannot let terrorists and rogue nations hold this nation hostile or hold our allies hostile.*'

✳

'*All I can tell you is when the governor calls, I answer his phone.*'

See also AND; GET.

Loved by crossword compilers, anagrams are the inevitable consequence of a language with more than 250,000 different words and only 26 letters. Take all the letters of a word or phrase, rearrange them to form another word or phrase and that's an anagram. Here are some examples:

angered ☛ ENRAGED
decanter ☛ CANTERED
deductions ☛ DISCOUNTED
orchestra ☛ CARTHORSE

The first example is known as a synanagram: an anagram whereby both parts are synonyms. Here's another famous example:

eleven plus two ☛ TWELVE PLUS ONE

Anagram fans have coined a number of words of their own for the different types of anagram. The opposite of a synanagram is called an antigram, where both parts are antonymous:

united ☛ UNTIED
misfortune ☛ IT'S MORE FUN
within earshot ☛ I WON'T HEAR THIS
sweltering heat ☛ THE WINTER GALES

Then there are pairagrams, where both parts have an association:

Elvis ☛ LIVES
married ☛ ADMIRER
best ☛ BETS
direct ☛ CREDIT

More complicated than this are trianagrams, which are three anagrammatical words or phrases:

mastering ☛ EMIGRANTS ☛ *streaming*
discounter ☛ INTRODUCES ☛ *reductions*

And more complicated still are anagrams of well-known phrases, which form a vague reference to the original phrase:

Rome was not built in a day
☞ ANY LABOUR I DO WANTS TIME.

A stitch in time saves nine
☞ IS THIS MEANT AS INCENTIVE?

Some celebrities' names make good anagrams:

ADOLF HITLER *Heil, old fart!* ✳ MONICA LEWINSKY *nice, silky woman* ✳ CLINT EASTWOOD *Old West action* ✳ YASMIN LE BON *mainly bones* ✳ ERIC CLAPTON *narcoleptic* ✳ BRITNEY SPEARS *Presbyterian* ✳ CAMILLA PARKER BOWLES *workable caramel lips* ✳ GLORIA ESTEFAN *large, fat noise* ✳ NAOMI CAMPBELL *blame, complain* ✳ SHARON STONE *no near shots* ✳ GILLIAN ANDERSON *no aliens, darling* ✳ PAUL MCCARTNEY *pay Mr Clean-cut* ✳ PLACIDO DOMINGO *God, I do complain* ✳ MARIE OSMOND *Mormon ideas* ✳ GEORGE W. BUSH *begs huge row*

But real anagram show-offs go further still, making anagrams of whole passages, with the new version having some reference to the old:

'*To be or not to be: that is the question; whether 'tis nobler in the mind to suffer the slings and arrows of outrageous fortune, or to take arms against a sea of troubles and by opposing, end them?*'

▼

'IS A BEFITTING QUOTE FROM ONE OF SHAKESPEARE'S GREATEST TRAGEDIES. BUT WHY WON'T HAMLET'S INSPIRING MOTTO TOSS OUR STUBBORN HERO'S TORTUOUS BATTLE FOR LIFE, ON ONE HAND, AND DEATH, ON ANOTHER?'

'And' is the only word in the English language to be regularly written as a symbol. The *&* symbol was formed by the Romans as a merger of the letters 'e' and 't' from *et*, the Latin word for 'and'. It is called an ampersand, which is a corruption of the phrase 'and per se and'. Per se is Latin for 'by itself', and this phrase used to be applied in schools for any letter of the alphabet that was a word in its own right: for example, 'a' and 'I'. The & symbol was included in recitals of the alphabet and so was referred to as 'and per se and', which, said quickly, becomes 'ampersand'.

'And' is also the fourth most commonly used word in English, or the third, depending on which source you believe. And, of course, the count is always changing and changing and changing. See, I've just upped the 'and' count in one sentence. And there's another. And another...

Brought into English by the Germanic tribes, from the same root that gives the German *und*, this versatile conjunction is a word that you would think every English speaker could use quite confidently and yet there is doubt over some of the rules associated with it. For example, can you start a sentence with 'and'?

Because 'and' is a conjunction and conjunctions connect words and clauses, there is an argument that it cannot begin a sentence because it is not connecting any parts of that sentence. This is an example of misguided rules cramping the style of good English. Obviously 'and' at the beginning of a sentence connects the sentence to the one or ones before. In that case, it is argued, the two sentences should become one, with 'and' joining them. But this would affect the pace of reading, negating the effect of the longer pause between sentences.

AND WHAT ABOUT THIS?

> 'And did those feet in ancient time
> Walk upon England's
> mountains green?'

In *Jerusalem*, William Blake begins with 'And', conjoining the first line with, well, nothing. Here the word 'and' is used in a similar way to the 'well' you often hear at the beginning of songs, beginning a narrative by giving the sense that it is a continuation of some bigger story.

The other dubious rule concerns the use of commas before 'and', especially in a list. Should it be *The Lion, the Witch and the Wardrobe* or *The Lion, the Witch, and the Wardrobe*? C.S. Lewis went with the former, although strict grammarians insist on the latter, arguing that it avoids ambiguity. Take this sentence: 'I remember the blue skies, the green fields and lakes.' Are the lakes green? Probably not, but we can't be sure. A comma before the 'and' would make this clear. The pro-comma lobby argues that making this a rule removes all doubt. Yet the modern convention is to regard 'and' as a replacement for the comma before the last item in a sequence. But we can still use a comma when required to avoid ambiguity: 'I remember the blue skies, the green fields, and lakes.' Job done.

And & to

An interesting use of 'and' is in place of 'to' in phrases like 'I'm going to try and find my coat.' The missing 'to' is actually part of the infinitive 'to find'. The origin is unclear, but the job it's doing is to tell us that the same form is applied as to the previous verb – a kind of verbal ditto mark.

infinitive ✳ *I'm going to try and find* ✳ *I'm going to try to find*
past ✳ *She went and found* ✳ *She went, she found*
future ✳ *I'll go and find* ✳ *I'll go, I'll find*
conditional ✳ *I could go and find* ✳ *I could go, I could find*

See also AMERICANISM; CONJUNCTION.

ANIMALS

Most of the English words for domesticated animals come from Anglo-Saxon. But the words we use for their meat come from French, which was introduced by the Normans after 1066.

Animal	Meat	French
CALF	veal	veau
COW	beef	boeuf
DEER	venison	venaison
PIG	pork	porc
SHEEP	mutton	mouton

The theory as to why this should have come about is that the poor farmers who tended the livestock were of Anglo-Saxon descent and, therefore, used the Old English words, whereas those who were served the meat without having to get involved in its slaughter were the wealthy Normans. However, Robert Burchfield states in his book *The English Language* that this 'is no more than a half truth'. He points out that both the French and the Anglo-Saxon terms were used for the animal and the meat up to the 18th century, although the examples he gives come from Dr Johnson and William Cowper, both highly educated men and, therefore, likely to use the French vocabulary.

The words for the young of domesticated animals are a whole creative field of their own. While calf, foal, chick, pup and cub are widely used for large mammals, equines, birds, canines and felines respectively, there are many animals whose young go by their own specific name. These are some of the more familiar examples:

CAT ♦	kitten ♦	*variant of old French* chitoun, *meaning 'small cat'*
DEER ♦	fawn ♦	*variant of old French* faon, *meaning 'young animal'*
DUCK ♦	duckling ♦	*diminutive of duck*
EEL ♦	elver ♦	*variant of 'eel-fare', an old term for a brood of young eels*
GOAT ♦	kid ♦	*from Old Norse for 'young goat'*
GOOSE ♦	gosling ♦	*diminutive form of Middle English 'gos', meaning 'goose'*
HARE ♦	leveret ♦	*from French* lièvre, *meaning hare*
KANGAROO ♦	joey ♦	*from native Australian name Joé*
SHEEP ♦	lamb ♦	*from German* Lamm
SWAN ♦	cygnet ♦	*from old French* cygne, *meaning 'swan'*

The question of whether animals have their own language divides opinion. Take whale song, bird song or the screech of baboons – all clearly carry a message. But do animals in different places have different accents? If not, why do the onomatopoeic words we use for the sounds they make differ from one language to another?

Animal	English	French	German	Japanese
CAT	meow	miaou	miau	nyaa
COCKEREL	cockadoodledoo	cocorico	kikeriki	kokekokko
COW	moo	meuh	muh	moo
DOG	woof-woof	ouah-ouah	wau-wau	wan-wan
DUCK	quack-quack	coin-coin	quaak-quaak	ga-ga
PIG	oink	groin-groin	grunz	buu-buu

An antonym is a word that is opposite in meaning to another word. So 'light' is the antonym of 'dark', 'tall' the antonym of 'short'. These two are examples of gradable antonyms; words which are at the opposite ends of a scale. They can, however, be modified, for example 'quite dark', 'very dark'.

Antonyms that are not gradable are called complementary antonyms. 'Alive' and 'dead', for example.

Some antonyms are not opposites, as such, but are distinct pairs in a relationship, for example 'husband' and 'wife', 'master' and 'servant'. These are called relational antonyms.

And then there are some words that can have two meanings in direct conflict with one another. 'Fast', for example, can mean rapid, or it can mean motionless, as in 'stuck fast'. 'Cleave' can mean to split or to join together. Words such as these are auto-antonyms.

Where a word does not have an antonym, one can be made by adding a negative prefix such as the Germanic 'un', the Latin 'in', or the Greek 'a'.

sure ♦♦♦ unsure   decent ♦♦♦ indecent   moral ♦♦♦ amoral

A feature of 21st century English is the use of 'not' in place of antonyms, for example 'I am so not happy about this.' It suggests an inability (antonym of ability) to come up with the right word, although it does carry a degree of emphasis that many more succinct antonyms lack.

See also So; SYNONYM.

APOSTROPHE

Apostrophe is a word of Greek origin. *Apo* meaning 'away from' is combined with *strephein*, meaning 'to turn' or 'to twist', to indicate that something has been taken away. One meaning of apostrophe is a dramatic exclamation or appeal to somebody or something, which interrupts the train of speech, such as Lady Macbeth's 'Out, damned spot! Out I say!' But most of us know an apostrophe as a punctuation mark – arguably the most misused of all punctuation marks – that indicates possession or the absence of a letter or letters.

> *'My dog's got no nose.'* (absent letter) *My dog has got no nose.*
> *'My dog's nose is missing.'* (possessive) *The nose of my dog is missing.*

In fact, when indicating possession the apostrophe is also replacing a missing letter. In Old English, possession was denoted by adding 'es' to the end of the noun. This was later abbreviated to 's' and an apostrophe added to mark the omission of the 'e' and distinguish the possessive from the plural. In German, which does not add 's' to the end of nouns to make them plural, no apostrophe is used to denote possession, since there is no confusion between a possessive and a plural.

So mistreated is the apostrophe in the English language that many books have been written in a bid to tackle the subject and sort it out once and for all. There is even an Apostrophe Protection Society (APS), which was established in London in 2001 'with the specific aim of preserving the correct use of this currently much abused punctuation mark in all forms of text written in the English language'.

The most common misuse of apostrophes involves the words 'its' and 'it's'. This is the correct use:

> *'It's got no nose.'* Apostrophe replaces 'has': *'It has got no nose.'*
> *'Its nose is missing'* Its with no apostrophe is a possessive pronoun.

It's (it is) easy to understand why this form confuses so many people. 'Its nose is missing' is possessive, right? And possessives take an apostrophe, right?

Wrong. Possessive nouns take an apostrophe, possessive pronouns do not. These are possessive pronouns:

HIS ❖ HERS ❖ OURS ❖ YOURS ❖ THEIRS ❖ ITS

 The next hurdle to get over is understanding where to put the apostrophe. A common mistake is to put it after the 's' when the noun is singular and before the 's' when the noun is plural.

'The dog's nose is missing.' The nose of the dog is missing.
'The dogs' nose is missing.' The nose of the dogs is missing.

Why more than one dog would share a nose is anyone's guess, but you get the point. The rule is simple: the apostrophe should come after the entire noun. To check that you're doing it correctly, turn the sentence round as above: is it 'The nose of the dog' or 'The nose of the dogs'? Put your apostrophe after 'dog' or 'dogs' accordingly.

Many people get confused when the plural form of a noun doesn't end with an 's', for example 'children' or 'people'. The tendency is to indicate the possessive form by adding an apostrophe after the added 's', for example childrens', peoples'. This is wrong. It should be 'children's' and 'people's' because the words 'children' and 'people' are already plural.

Nouns that end in 's' are doubly confusing. Names like Jones (plural: Joneses), for example, can lead to all sorts of apostrophic nightmares. But hold your nerve, remember to check what the noun is and add your apostrophes in the correct manner.

> *'I went to Mrs Jones' house.'* I went to the house of Mrs Jones.
> *'I went to the Joneses' house.'* I went to the house of the Joneses.

You could write these as 'Mrs Jones's house' and 'the Joneses's house', it's up to you. When the noun, singular or plural, ends in 's', it is not necessary to add the extra 's' after the apostrophe, though some people prefer to as it reflects their pronunciation.

The APS also states that apostrophes should never be used to make things plural. And in this it faces probably its toughest battle. Just pay a visit to your local greengrocer's (if you still have one) to see the strength of the enemy.

Greengrocers	APS	Greengrocers	APS
banana's	bananas	pizza's	pizzas
mango's	mangos	satsuma's	satsumas

All the greengrocers' examples are common abuses of the apostrophe, but understandable if used to aid pronunciation. For example, without the apostrophe we might all go about sounding like Spaniards, asking for 'mangoss' and 'satsumass'. So shouldn't we be allowed some dispensation for stretching the rules of apostrophe use in cases where it helps us to understand what is meant?

The Oxford English Dictionary sanctions the use of an apostrophe when pluralizing lower case letters as in, for example, 'There are four i's in Mississippi.' Otherwise it would be, 'There are four is in Mississippi'? The *OED* also apostrophizes 'do's, as in 'do's and don'ts', but this is frowned upon by the APS. Dos and don'ts are all very well, but say the word 'dos' on its own and it's likely to come out as 'doss'.

'Panting for it' might strike you as a slightly vulgar way of saying eagerly desiring, but it is true to the origins of the more refined 'aspiring'. Derived from the Latin *spirare* (to breathe) – from which we also get 'inspire', 'expire', 'respirator', etc. – with the prefix 'ad' (to), aspiration in the sense of ambition means breathing desire for.

Aspiration is also the physical process by which certain consonants, such as 'k', 'p' and 't' are pronounced. These consonants in words like 'key', 'peak' and 'tone' involved a sharp outflow of breath (aspiration). Put an 's' in front and they are pronounced without the aspiration. Try it by holding your hand in front of your mouth and saying the following:

key *ski* ♦ peak *speak* ♦ tone *stone*

Aspiration is closely associated with the letter 'h'. 'H' is an aspirated consonant in 'hot' and 'hatch' but is silent in 'hour' and 'honour'.

See also WHY.

ASSONANCE

Not to be confused with alliteration, assonance is the repetition of vowel sounds within words that end in different consonants. It is a poetic device, sometimes confused with rhyme, the difference being that rhyming words also end in the same consonant. Here are two examples:

'Sign of the times' the 'i' sound in 'sign' and 'times'.
'Love is the drug' the 'u' sound in 'love' and 'drug'.

Similar to assonance is consonance, which is the repetition of consonant sounds but with different vowels, for example 'zigger-zagger'.

See also ALLITERATION; CONSONANT; RHYME; VOWEL.

BOWDLERIZE

A verb meaning to censor by taking out all the rude words or offensive references, Bowdlerize is an eponym after Dr Thomas Bowdler (1754–1825). He made his name by producing *The Family Shakespeare* in 1818, which contained all 37 of Shakespeare's plays with any obscenity, sexual indelicacy and blasphemy edited out. Or, in Bowdler's words, 'those words and expressions are omitted which cannot with propriety be read aloud in a family.' Interestingly, Bowdler was happy to let the violence go. Bowdler's work (actually started by his sister Henrietta, though she remained uncredited) has been both derided and praised but not ignored. It helped to encourage the learning of Shakespeare among children in the 19th century. And Bowdlerization is commonplace in the modern music business, in which edited versions of numerous songs are produced to comply with the daytime airplay censorship laws.

BRAND

> *'A brand is a living entity... the product of a thousand small gestures.'*
>
> Michael Eisner, CEO The Walt Disney Company 1984–2005

Derived from the practice of marking livestock with a hot iron, the word brand is now most commonly associated with the marketing of consumer goods. Just as cattle needed to be branded in order to distinguish whose were whose, so manufacturers found they needed to do the same with their goods in order to mark them out in an increasingly crowded market.

It began in the 19th century, when industrialization saw an increase in packaged goods, produced in central factories and shipped to far-flung markets. In order to win the trust of new customers more accustomed to buying local goods, they had to create a sense of familiarity, which they did by stamping the product name on the packaging in a recognizable style. Pears Soap, launched in 1789, claims to be the world's first registered brand. Still essentially about gaining consumers' trust and loyalty, the business of branding has become a major factor in modern retail, to the extent that many companies value their brand identity more than the actual company itself. There is no greater sign of successful branding than when the brand becomes adopted as a generic word, synonymous with the product.

HERE ARE TEN OF THE MOST FAMOUS BRANDS TO HAVE
ACHIEVED THIS EXALTED STATUS.

❶ ASPIRIN headache pill ❷ BIRO ballpoint pen ❸ DUREX contraceptive sheath ❹ GOOGLE Internet search (to Google) ❺ HOOVER vacuum cleaner (to hoover) ❻ KLEENEX tissue ❼ SELLOTAPE adhesive tape ❽ TARMAC road surfacing ❾ THERMOS vacuum flask ❿ XEROX photocopier (to xerox)

Admittedly Xerox has faded from common usage since the 1970s, but Hoover retains its place in the lexicon despite the company losing its dominance of the vacuum cleaner market. Biro became a genericized trademark in 1950, when László Bíró sold the patent for his ballpoint pen to Marcel Bich, who marketed it as the Bic Biro.

See also EPONYM.

BREWER, REVD DR EBENEZER COBHAM (1810-1897)

In 1870 E. Cobham Brewer, a clergyman, schoolmaster and author who described himself as a 'snapper-up of unconsidered trifles', produced a dictionary that would become the most popular source of explanation of phrases, proper names and words 'that have a tale to tell'. The

Dictionary of Phrase and Fable, now known affectionately as 'Brewer's', contains some 20,000 entries and was most recently updated in 2005.

The preface to the first edition summed up the contents thus:
'It draws in curious or novel etymologies, pseudonyms and popular titles, local traditions and literary blunders, biographical and historical trifles too insignificant to find a place in books of higher pretension, but not too worthless to be worth knowing.'

See also DICTIONARY.

BUZZ WORD

'Man is a creature who lives not upon bread alone,
but primarily by catchwords.'
Robert Louis Stevenson

Closely allied to brands and marketing, a buzz word is a term used to convey the impression of being 'in the know' while actually having little or no relevant meaning. In short, it is used to impress rather than to inform.

Buzzword Bingo (aka Bullshit) is a popular game in business meetings, whereby you have a list of buzz words and every time you hear one mentioned you cross it off. The first person to cross off all their words shouts 'Bingo!' or, if they're feeling brave, 'Bullshit!' and wins the prize. Try it yourself with these buzz words.

✳ *ask (noun, as in 'big ask')* ✳ *implement* ✳ *ballpark* ✳ *interface* ✳ *connectivity* ✳ *leverage* ✳ *diversity* ✳ *organic* ✳ *dynamic* ✳ *proactive* ✳ *empower* ✳ *scalable* ✳ *envelope* ✳ *synergy* ✳ *ethos* ✳ *task (verb)* ✳ *framework* ✳ *transparency* ✳ *grow (transitive)* ✳ *whammy*

See also CLICHÉ; JARGON.

BYWORD

The most common use of 'byword' in modern English is as a synonym or epithet, a name or expression that represents something more general. For example, Rolls-Royce is a byword for quality.

But a byword is also a proverb, saying or slogan.

THE C WORD

As four-letter words go, none can match the offensive power of 'the C word'; which is precisely why I'm referring to it as 'the C word'. This piece of Anglo-Saxon mischief has been around in the English language since the 13th century, according to the *Oxford English Dictionary*, but we still haven't grown accustomed to it. Why it should have remained so taboo for 800 years is difficult to explain, but while 'the F word' has become commonplace in popular culture, to the point of overuse, 'the C word' remains beyond the pale.

In fact, the *OED* refused to list it until 1972; so obscene is it, so offensive that even today most people can only bring themselves to refer to it as 'the C word', or in code, for example 'C U Next Tuesday'.

The C word is regarded as the most indelicate of all names for the female genitals, which is saying something.

In 2000 a survey was carried out in Britain with the aim of gauging public attitudes to obscene language. *Delete Expletives?* graded a list of profanities in order of severity. Amongst the 'very severe' were terms of racial abuse, abuse of minorities and directive abuse. You don't have to think too hard to see how all these terms cause severe offence, yet top of the list came the C word.

The only conclusion we can draw is that it's not the literal meaning alone that causes offence. If it was, other expressions would be deemed equally offensive, but they're not. Why aren't other rude words on a par? More likely it's to do with the ugly pronunciation of the word; the 'un' combination seems to be designed for ugly words:

BRUNT ◆ DUNG ◆ GRUNT ◆ RUNT

This jars with our preferred perception of the female genitals – they should be handled more sensitively. Nevertheless, a catalogue of eminent and sensitive writers, including Samuel Beckett, James Joyce, George Orwell and D.H. Lawrence, have plumped for the C word, no doubt enjoying its literary power to leap off the page.

But none of them managed to extract as much from the word as Peter Cook and Dudley Moore who, in a legendary sketch entitled 'This Bloke Came Up to Me', featuring their alter egos Derek and Clive, managed 28 mentions of the C word in a mere 1 minute 22 seconds.

See also EXPLETIVE; THE F WORD; FOUR-LETTER WORDS; PROFANITY.

CARROLL, LEWIS (1832-1898)

Lewis Carroll was the pseudonym of English writer Charles Lutwidge Dodgson. The pen name was a derivation of his own, Lewis being an anglicized version of Ludovicus, the Latin root of Lutwidge, and Carroll coming from Carolus; Charles in Latin.

Dodgson was that rarity, a man with a highly proficient grasp of both words and numbers, although he spoke with a stammer and found children easier to converse with than adults. His most famous works, *Alice's Adventures in Wonderland* (1865) and *Through the Looking Glass and What Alice Found There* (1872), were written for Alice Liddell, daughter of the dean of Christ Church College, Oxford, where Dodgson lectured in mathematics for 26 years.

He wrote several books on mathematics, as well as politics and other serious matters, but it's his stories and poems for children that live on today. He was one of the finest exponents of the art of neologism, the coining of new words. In his famous poem 'Jabberwocky', which appears in *Through the Looking Glass*, one word in four is a Carroll invention, including 'burbled', 'galumphing' and 'chortled', which have all entered the dictionary.

'Twas brillig, and the slithy toves
Did gyre and gimble in the wabe:
All mimsy were the borogoves,
And the mome raths outgrabe.'

'Beware the Jabberwock, my son!
The jaws that bite, the claws that catch!
Beware the Jubjub bird, and shun
The frumious Bandersnatch!'

He took his vorpal sword in hand:
Long time the manxome foe he sought -
So rested he by the Tumtum tree,
And stood awhile in thought.

And, as in uffish thought he stood,
The Jabberwock, with eyes of flame,
Came whiffling through the tulgey wood,
And burbled as it came!

One, two! One, two! And through and through
The vorpal blade went snicker-snack!
He left it dead, and with its head
He went galumphing back.

'And, hast thou slain the Jabberwock?
Come to my arms, my beamish boy!
O frabjous day! Callooh! Callay!'
He chortled in his joy.

'Twas brillig, and the slithy toves
Did gyre and gimble in the wabe;
All mimsy were the borogoves,
And the mome raths outgrabe.'

These are examples of 'portmanteau' words, a term which was also coined by Carroll in *Through the Looking Glass*. The character Humpty Dumpty explains it best when talking about the word 'slithy'. 'It's like a portmanteau,' he says. 'There are two meanings packed up into one word.' In the case of  slithy, the two words are 'lithe' and 'slimy'; chortle is a combination of 'chuckle' and 'snort'; galumphing a blend of 'galloping' and 'triumph'.

Many of the words Carroll created for 'Jabberwocky' also appear in his nonsense poem 'The Hunting of the Snark' (1876), which indicates that he clearly knew what these, if not all of his neologisms, meant in his own mind. 'Beamish', 'uffish', 'galumphing' and 'outgrabe' are all there, plus an appearance of the Jubjub bird and the 'frumious Bandersnatch'. The skill of Carroll's writing means that the reader also gains a clear impression of the scene being depicted and it illustrates how the sound of words can be as powerful as their meaning in painting vivid pictures.

See also NEOLOGISM; PORTMANTEAU.

CASE

The word 'case' has two meanings relevant to words. In typography, upper case and lower case are alternative ways of saying capitals and small letters, more of which in a minute. In grammatical terms, the case of a noun, pronoun or adjective describes its position within the sentence. Latin has six cases and Finnish 15 while the unfortunate learner of Hungarian is faced with more than 25.

Anyone who has studied Latin will perhaps have memories of wrestling with the declensions of nouns in their different cases (nominative, genitive, dative, accusative, ablative, vocative), but the English speaker can take heart. English, by contrast, relies on prepositions, word order and the dreaded apostrophe for clarity.

According to Fowler, '... English had once case-forms for nouns as well as pronouns [but] found them of... little use...'. However, even though pronouns have retained the Old English habit of changing form according to their case, this part of English grammar is very familiar to the English speaker, as you will see.

Singular			
nominative	I	you	he/she/it
genitive	my/mine	your/yours	his/her/hers/its
dative	me	you	him/her/it
accusative	me	you	him/her/it
reflexive	myself	yourself	himself/herself/itself

Plural			
nominative	we	you	they
genitive	our/ours	your/yours	their/theirs
dative	us	you	them
accusative	us	you	them
reflexive	ourselves	yourselves	themselves

When it comes to the pronoun 'who/whom', though, uncertainty reigns. In fact, the rule is simple: 'who' is the subject case (nominative), 'whom' is the object case (accusative/dative). So in the sentence:

> *'Who did what to whom?'*

'Who' is the person doing, 'whom' is the person being done to. The problem for 'whom' is that it has become regarded, wrongly, as just a quaint alternative to 'who', rather like among and amongst or while and whilst, and speakers who prefer modern English have tended to abandon it. In fairness, it is not essential to the sense of a sentence and purists are having to fight hard to preserve its use.

For example, 'I know who you're going out with,' is perfectly clear, even though it should be, 'I know whom you're going out with.'

A simple way to check whether it should be 'who' or 'whom' is to substitute the word for 'he' or 'him' and reorder the sentence accordingly.

> *'You're going out with he.'* WRONG
> *'You're going out with him.'* RIGHT

Where 'him' is correct, use 'whom'. Where 'he' is correct', use 'who'. And don't forget the possessive case is 'whose' (genitive), not who's.

The other use of the word 'case', for capital (majuscule) and small (minuscule) letters, comes from the print business. The letters were kept in the cases or drawers of a cabinet and because the minuscule letters were used more often, they were kept in the lower case; the less frequently used majuscule letters were kept in the upper case. Simple as that.

Originally the alphabet was only upper case, the development of minuscule writing taking place between the 3rd and the 12th centuries AD as a method of writing more quickly. The first standard was the Carolingian Minuscule, developed under the auspices of Emperor Charlemagne in the 8th century. This spread throughout Western Europe and by the time Johannes Gutenberg invented printing with moveable type, minuscule lettering had become the norm, with majuscule letters being used to begin sentences and pick out nouns.

The use of upper case letters in modern English is now restricted to the initial letters of proper nouns such as John, London and England, acronyms like NATO and USA and, occasionally, emphasis: 'I will NOT tell you again!'

A common mistake is to write the names of the seasons with upper case initial letters, but they should be written winter, spring, summer and autumn (fall). Titles should only take a capital letter when written as part of the name. This example shows the distinction:

'Queen Elizabeth II of England' BUT *'Elizabeth II, the queen of England'*.

See also I; NOUN.

CLICHÉ

'It is a cliché that most clichés are true, but then like most clichés, that cliché is untrue.'
Stephen Fry

The word cliché was given to us by the French and a proper Trojan Horse it has proven to be. Like 'case', it comes from printing. Stereotype printing is where a plate is cast by dipping a mould of the lettering or image to be printed into molten metal. The French gave this dipping the onomatopoeic word *clicher*, *cliché* being the past participle. So, put simply, a cliché is an expression that has been cast in metal, that is made permanent.

One of the most common yet most maligned uses of words, a cliché could be defined as a phrase or saying that is so overused as to render the user liable to physical assault. That's not the OED definition, but it does convey the sense of disdain that clichés seem to engender. Why this should be is anyone's guess. There you go, I just did it myself. Clichés are so convenient and easy to use, so why all the fuss? Sure, they may be the lazy option in sentence construction, but we can't all be William Shakespeare. Are we all expected to be so erudite that we can get through life without ever uttering one of these clichéd favourites:

Beauty is only skin deep ✦ *He had a good innings* ✦ *He's his own worst enemy* ✦ *I'm only human* ✦ *If you can't beat them, join them* ✦ *It could be worse* ✦ *It's the thought that counts* ✦ *Life goes on* ✦ *No pain, no gain* ✦ *No rest for the wicked* ✦ *Nobody's perfect* ✦ *One step at a time* ✦ *That's life* ✦ *There are plenty more fish in the sea* ✦ *Tomorrow's another day* ✦ *Two steps forward, one step back* ✦ *Worse things happen at sea* ✦ *You live and learn* ✦ *You're making a rod for your own back*

Many of these clichés fall into the subsets of platitudes and truisms. A platitude is a cliché delivered with a certain solemnity, while the very fact that the words are not original undermines its apparent sincerity. 'It's the thought that counts' and 'He had a good innings' are examples.

A truism is a cliché that is so obviously true as to be not worth uttering. 'Tomorrow's another day.' Really? You don't say.

What is most important when resorting to clichés is to remain aware of the original meaning of the phrases. Sometimes they are trotted out in situations for which they are not ideally suited. There is a soccer pundit in England who is fond of the expression, 'Indecision is final.' A cliché all of his own, this is

presumably a hybrid of two other clichés, 'Indecision is fatal' and 'The referee's decision is final'. This takes us towards the point at which clichés do start to rankle. In the business world (and that includes politics and sport), newly coined clichés go hand in hand with buzz words as the modern way of trying to appear knowledgeable while saying nothing of any value. Try adding these to your Buzzword Bingo cards:

Get our ducks in a row ✱ *Pick the low-hanging fruit* ✱ *Run it up the flagpole and see who salutes* ✱ *Sing from the same hymn sheet* ✱ *Think outside the box*

It's worth stating, in their defence, that most clichés are good, evocative metaphors and whoever first came up with them deserves credit (Shakespeare, for example). They paint a mental picture that is perfectly clear and easy to grasp. The fault lies with those of us who pick them up and try to make them our own. It's the same mistake as quoting lines from *Monty Python* and thinking that makes you a comedian.

See also BUZZ WORD; SAYINGS; SHAKESPEARE

COMPOUND

A word formed by putting two words together is a compound word. Examples include:

handbag ✦ *letterbox* ✦ *newspaper*

These examples are all combinations of two nouns. Some compounds combine nouns and adjectives and are often hyphenated, for example lazy-bones, big-head. Others combine nouns and verbs as in skydiving and handmade.

A rich source of compounds is the legal profession, which loves to use compounded adverbial conjunctions:

> *albeit* ♦ *hereafter* ♦ *however*
> ♦ *moreover* ♦ *nevertheless*
> ♦ *nonetheless* ♦ *notwithstanding*

Some of these, you'll notice, are triple compound words – combinations of three words. Here are some more:

> *hereinafter* ♦ *inasmuch*
> ♦ *wherewithal* ♦ *whosoever*

According to the *Oxford English Dictionary*, 'inasmuch' is a compound word whereas its synonym 'in so far' is not. Yeah, like, whatever!

Compounding is an ongoing process in the English language and if enough people write 'insofar' as one word, as they do, it is bound to become one. The same is true of 'alright' and 'eachother'.

Some compounds are not completely unified but are held together by a hyphen:

> *side-table* (noun) ♦ *home-made* (adjective) ♦ *water-ski* (verb)

The hyphen enables us to make compounds at will, especially compound adjectives and adverbs. In, for example, 'fast-moving film' it is necessary to indicate that the action is fast-moving, as opposed to fast and moving.

However, a lot of style guides advocate a hyphen to form compound adjectives like 'rapidly-flowing river', 'quickly-taken penalty', etc., but this is unnecessary. 'Rapidly' is clearly an adverb and, therefore, must describe the verb 'flowing', rather than the noun 'river'. There is no ambiguity so there is no need for the hyphen. In fact, there's no need to call it a compound adjective.

See also ADVERB; CONJUNCTION; CONTRACTION; HYPHEN.

COMPUTER LANGUAGE

The onset of the computer age has seen us endowed with a whole new vocabulary. Bits, bytes, chips and PINs, e-mail, Internet, cyberspace, hypertext, WAP and Wi-Fi... Thankfully you don't have to learn all of these terms in order to work a computer, but many of them have nevertheless filtered into the English language and are now common usage. We think nothing of talking about our SIM card, although we may not know that SIM stands for Subscriber Identity Module.

But this hi-tech jargon is just the tip of the iceberg. Somewhere in a hushed office near you, hidden behind a door marked 'IT Dept', they're speaking in a language designed for nobody else to understand. Stumble in there in the hope of finding somebody who can clean the coffee out of your keyboard and you can expect to be bombarded with 'words' such as USB, driver, firewall, Ethernet, DOS and idiot. So that you feel a little more confident next time this happens, here's a quick glossary of useful computer geek terms.

APPLICATION A software program, for example word processing, graphic design or Internet browser.

ATTACHMENT A file sent by e-mail.

AVATAR An image used to represent a person online, for example in an Internet forum.

BANDWIDTH The amount of data transferred by a website over a given period of time.

BIT The smallest unit of information in a computer.

BLOG Short for weblog, a personal documentation of thoughts and experiences on a website.

BYTE Unit of information required to store one character – the equivalent of 8 bits.

COOKIE A data file placed on your PC by a website, ostensibly so it can remember your preferences, for example log in details. But some also gather data such as which adverts you've seen.

CYBERSPACE The Internet universe.

DOMAIN An Internet address.

The bit that ends .com or whatever.

DONGLE A small device that must be plugged into a computer before it can run certain software.

EMOTICON One of a group of symbols used in e-mail or texting to portray emotion, for example :-) (smiley), ;-) (wink) and :-0 (gasp). Also known as smileys.

ETHERNET A type of network, or a system for connecting computers to form a network.

EXTENSION The part of a file name that comes after the dot, denoting what type of file it is, for example .jpg (jpeg), .ppt (powerpoint).

FAQ Frequently asked questions.

FIREWALL A program or a feature built into hardware which protects a computer or network from net-borne attacks.

HACKER Somebody who gains unauthorized access to computer files via the Internet or other networks.

IDIOT Somebody who spills coffee on their keyboard.

IP ADDRESS Short for Internet Protocol, this is the unique identity number that every machine attached to the Internet needs to ensure the data it requests returns to the right place.

KILLER APP A fantastically useful software program.

NETIQUETTE Good practice when using the Internet.

PODCAST An audio file that can be downloaded to a computer or portable music player.

POP-UP An Internet browser window that opens separately to the main window, usually used for advertising.

PORT The virtual door through which data from the Internet enters a PC.

PROTOCOL A set of rules that allows computers to exchange information, not a language – although a language might be specified in a protocol.

RAM Short for Random Access Memory, the main memory supporting whatever you're working on, which becomes inactive when the computer is shut down.

ROM Short for Read Only Memory, containing preset information intended to remain unchanged.

SERVER A computer that provides services to others on a network.

SPAM Mass distribution of e-mails usually containing advertising. Spam is not an acronym – the term comes from *Monty Python*.

STREAM Video or audio file that plays while it downloads.

VIRUS A malicious program, usually requiring action to successfully infect a victim.

WEBSPACE The space on a server where websites are kept.

WI-FI Wireless system of connecting computers to a network.

WYSIWYG Pronounced 'wizzywig', it stands for what you see is what you get and describes software that presents an accurate visual representation of the end product on screen.

Delve into the murky world of cybercrime and the vocabulary expands further still. As with all languages, the high-tech criminal fraternity contributes generously to the slang of the genre. As we all try to guard against our identities and our possessions being filched via our phone line as we lie in our beds at night, prepare to find the following

terms cropping up again and again.

BLACKHAT Hackers with criminal or malicious intentions, for example writers of destructive viruses and those that steal financial data.

BOTNET A number of hijacked computers (bots, from 'robot') under the remote control of a single person via the Internet. Bots are usually home PCs belonging to unsuspecting users, recruited via a virus sent by e-mail, or by drive-by downloads and worms.

BOTNET HERDER Someone who controls a botnet.

CARDER Someone who trades in stolen credit card numbers.

CASH-OUT To steal money from a bank account or credit card to which someone has gained illegal access.

DEAD-DROP A hijacked PC or server used to store all the

personal data stolen by keyloggers, spyware or viruses.

DDOS Short for Distributed Denial of Service, an attack in which thousands of separate computers bombard a target with bogus data to knock it off the net. Often used as a threat with a ransom demand.

DRIVE-BY DOWNLOAD Malicious programs that automatically install when a potential victim visits a booby-trapped website.

HONEYPOT A computer or network of computers that appear poorly protected but are set up to trap hackers.

KEYLOGGER A program installed on a victim's machine that records every keystroke they make. Used for stealing login and password details.

MALWARE Any malicious software.

PHISHING Sending out e-mail messages that seek to trick people into handing over confidential details.

ROOTS Networks that have been hacked into for malicious ends.

SPYWARE Malicious program that steals personal and confidential information.

TROJAN A program or message, often attached to an e-mail, that looks benign but conceals a malicious payload.

WHITEHAT A hacker who works for good, trying to thwart malicious hackers.

WORM A self-propelled malicious program that scours the web seeking new victims.

ZOMBIE Another name for a hijacked computer that is part of a botnet.

See also JARGON.

CONJUNCTION

A word that joins words or clauses in a sentence is a conjunction. 'And' and 'but' are the most common examples, but there are lots more. They come in three types: co-ordinating, subordinating and correlative.

THE CO-ORDINATING CONJUNCTIONS ARE:

and ✦ or ✦ but ✦ so ✦ for ✦ yet ✦ nor

SUBORDINATING CONJUNCTIONS INCLUDE:

after ✦ rather than ✦ although ✦ since ✦ as ✦ so that ✦ as if ✦ that ✦ as though ✦ unless ✦ because ✦ until ✦ before ✦ when ✦ if ✦ while ✦ once

---

They come at the beginning of subordinate clauses and establish the way in which the subordinate clause qualifies the main clause. In other words, they give the clause its meaning. Take this sentence:

'He always watched TV before he took a shower.'

Now change the conjunction 'before' and you get a very different statement.

'He always watched TV while he took a shower.'

OR

'He always watched TV unless he took a shower.'

That's the value of a subordinating conjunction.

Correlative conjunctions work in pairs. In the sentence, 'Neither Tom nor John was playing,' neither and nor are the correlative conjunctions. Note also the use of the singular verb 'was'. It is a common mistake to use a plural, 'were' in this instance. The two subjects are singular so a singular verb is needed. Other correlative conjunctions include:

as... *as* ✳ both... *and* ✳ either... *or* ✳ neither... *nor* ✳ not... *but* ✳ not only... *but also* ✳ whether... *or*

There is another group of words that work as conjunctions, in that they connect clauses within a sentence, or rather form a transition between clauses. They needn't be positioned at the end of a clause where the join occurs and so they are not actual conjunctions. 'However' is one. 'I like him; however, I don't trust him,' could also be written: 'I like him; I don't trust him, however.' These words are known as adverbial conjunctions and they include:

CONSEQUENTLY ✳ OTHERWISE ✳ HENCE SIMILARLY ✳ HOWEVER ✳ STILL ✳ MOREOVER ✳ THEREFORE ✳ NEVERTHELESS ✳ THUS

Notice the punctuation in the sample sentences in the previous paragraph. The clauses are separated with a semi-colon and the adverbial conjunction is separated from its clause with a comma. This is the correct way to

JOIN or DIE

punctuate adverbial conjunctions because the transition puts a break in the flow of the sentence, yet does not create a new one. Therefore, using a comma or a full stop in place of the semi-colon, as is the prevailing trend, is a poor use of punctuation.

See also AND.

CONSONANT

A consonant could be defined as a part of a word that isn't a vowel. However, that would require a definition of 'vowel', and we haven't come to 'v' yet. *The Oxford Reference Dictionary* defines a consonant as 'a speech sound in which the breath is at least partially obstructed, combining with a vowel to form a syllable'. The bit about 'combining with a vowel' hints at the word's derivation: 'con-sonant' comes from the Latin *consonare*, meaning 'sounding together', representing the notion that it needs a vowel sound before or after it to generate the breath to make it sound.

Interestingly, there are not enough consonants in the English alphabet (21 at the last count) to represent the consonant sounds in the language, so combinations of letters, called digraphs, are used to create sounds like 'ch', 'sh' and 'th'.

Consonants fall into four categories – stops, fricatives, approximants and nasals – according to the way they are sounded.

STOPS

✳ **B** of *ball* and *club* ✳ **D** of *dog* and *lead* ✳ **G** of *golf* and *bag* ✳ **C** of *cut* and *panic* + **K** of *kiss* and **CK** of *lick* ✳ **P** of *punch* and *rap* ✳ **T** of *time* and *minute* ✳ **SP** of *spoil* and *wasp* ✳ **ST** of *start* and *first* ✳ **SK** of *skid* and *risk*

Also among the stops are the 'flap t' sound of 'bitter' when prounced in the American style, almost as 'bidder', and the glottal stop in 'uh-uh'.

FRICATIVES

✳ **F** of *fang* and *wolf* + **PH** of *phonetic* and *graph* ✳ **H** of *hot* and *Sahara* ✳ **S** of *sad* and *loss* ✳ **S** of *leisure* and *measure* + **GE** of *rouge* and *gerberer* ✳ **V** of *veal* and *clove* ✳ **Z** of *zeal* and *crazy* ✳ **CH** of *chow* and

lunch ✳ **DG** *of grudge and dudgeon* + **J** *of justice* ✳ **TH** *of this and lithe*
✳ **TH** *of thick and* *both* ✳ **SH** *of shell and shore* + **CH** *of chamois and*
pastiche ✳ **W** *of what and where* (pronounced with an 'h' sound
before the 'w')

APPROXIMANTS

L of *lip* and *ledge* ✳ **R** of *red* and *robin* ✳ **W** of *wig* and *walrus* ✳ **Y** of
yellow and *yacht* ✳ **LL** of *belle* and *ball*

NASALS

M of *man* and *him* ❖ **N** of *naughty* and *sin* ❖ **NG** of *England* and *dreaming*

Within these categories consonants are further classified according to factors such as the degree of vocal chord vibration (for example 'z' a lot, 's' none) and where in the mouth the airflow is obstructed to create the sounds (for example the lips, tongue against top teeth).

The modern definition of a consonant is more complicated than simply saying it goes with a vowel to form a syllable. Some consonants manage to form a syllable without a vowel sound, such as the second syllable in 'cattle' and 'mutton', which could be written 'cattl' and 'muttn' and would still be pronounced the same. We now know that spoken consonants need a vowel sound as well, so you'd think that six consonants in a row between vowels would be a linguistic challenge. But that's just what happens in some English words. Take 'watchstrap' or 'catchphrase', for example. Such words are rarities, though. Much more common are words with five consecutive consonants:

BACKSTROKE ◆ BIRTHPLACE ◆ BREASTSTROKE ◆ CORKSCREW ◆
DRAUGHTSMAN ◆ ERSTWHILE ◆ JOCKSTRAP ◆ LENGTHWISE ◆ MATCHSTICK
◆ NIGHTCLUB ◆ POSTSCRIPT ◆ SWITCHBLADE ◆ WITCHCRAFT

See also GHOTI; PHONETICS; RHYTHM.

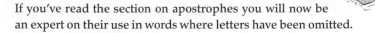

CONTRACTION

If you've read the section on apostrophes you will now be an expert on their use in words where letters have been omitted.

> *he'll* ● *he will*
> *it's* ● *it is/has*
> *can't* ● *cannot*
> *ne'er-do-well* ● *never-do-well*

It's very easy to see in these cases how the apostrophe replaces the missing letters. But what about this?

'I am making myself clear, aren't I?'

What is 'aren't I' short for in this instance? 'Are not I'? How can it be? 'Are' is not the first person singular of the verb 'to be'. We don't say 'I are', do we?

The truth is that 'aren't I' is snobbery gone mad. Back in the 17th century the grammatically correct but rather grandiose 'am not I' was abbreviated to 'an't I' (note, no apostrophe for the missing 'm').

This in turn produced the variant 'ain't', which is, of course, widely used today, although still regarded as slang. And it's this failure of the word 'ain't' to establish itself in polite company that led to polite company lengthening the 'ai' sound to an 'aah' sound and creating the monster that is 'aren't I'.

Rather than slipping away to die quietly in a back street of some London slum, 'ain't' fought back and widened its influence beyond the first person: 'he ain't', 'they ain't'; and even, in some dialects, beyond the verb 'to be': 'I ain't wanna come', meaning 'I don't want to come'.

An alternative way of saying this would be 'I won't come.' And this is another oddity. 'He won't' is surely short for 'he will not', so why the 'o'? The first recorded use of 'won't' is from the late 17th century, before which 'wonnot' had been used, a derivation of 'wynnot', which became the abbreviated way of saying 'will not' some time around 1550.

Another contraction that has undergone further transformation is the word 'till, most commonly used as an abbreviation of until. Just as 'tis became the abbreviation of 'it is' and ne'er the abbreviation of never, 'til was the quick and easy way to say until. Perhaps because it is used so often, whereas 'tis and ne'er are seldom seen outside the pages of the romantic poets, it has lost the rather uncomfortable apostrophe at the beginning and the awkward single 'l' at the end has been doubled up to give us 'till', which looks more like a proper word. 'Alright' also looks like a proper word. We see it often enough and say it even more often, but, in fact, 'alright' is not a word, according to the *Oxford English Dictionary*. It should be spelt out as 'all right'. 'Altogether' should only be used to mean 'entirely', for example 'That's a different matter altogether.' When referring to a number of people or things acting in unison, 'all together' is the correct form. The film *Airplane* made fun of this distinction in a scene where ex-airforce-pilot-turned-alcoholic Striker is being cajoled by the cabin crew into taking control of the plane.

▶ STRIKER: *'I flew single engine fighters in the Air Force, but this plane has four engines. It's an entirely different kind of flying altogether.'*

▶ ALL TOGETHER: *'It's an entirely different kind of flying.'*

DEFINITION

The *OED* definition of 'definition' is: 'A declaration or formal explanation of the signification of a word or phrase.' It comes, rather obviously, from the Latin definire, meaning to limit or mark out.

'Definition' is also used in relation to pictures, describing the clarity and distinctness of an image. Other related words that we use today include:

definite ▶▶ *definitive*
fine ▶▶ *finery*
finish ▶▶ *finite* ▶▶ *infinite* ▶▶ *infinity*
refine ▶▶ *refinery* ▶▶ *refinement*

DICTIONARY

'Dictionaries are like watches; the worst is better than none, and the best cannot be expected to go quite true.'
Samuel Johnson

Dictionaries have been with us in some shape or form for almost as long as we have been able to write. The Chinese and the Japanese had dictionaries long before Dr Samuel Johnson published *A Dictionary of the English Language*, which is considered the template for all modern dictionaries.

Johnson's was not the first dictionary to tackle the English language, though; far from it. That achievement is generally attributed to Sir Thomas Elyot, a scholarly knight in the court of King Henry VIII, who produced the *Latin Dictionary* in 1538. Most other dictionaries that followed at around that time were also designed for the purpose of translating other languages, French, German or Latin, into English.

But in 1604 a schoolteacher named Robert Cawdrey published *A Table Alphabeticall*. Cawdrey's book was a reaction to what he saw as a disturbing influx of foreign words into the English language, abetted by the burgeoning printing industry, and it set out not only to tackle this new vocabulary but also to protect the perfectly good words that were being ousted. Just as so many writers on the subject today grumble about the influx of 'Americanisms' into the English language, so Cawdrey made his feelings clear in his introduction to the reader. (Note the absence of the letters 'j' and 'v', still not included in the alphabet at that time.)

'*Some far iournied gentlemen, at their returne home, like as they loue to go in forraine apparrell, so they will pouder their talke with ouer-sea language. He that commeth lately out of France, will talk French English, and neuer blush at the matter.*'

'Powder their talk with overseas language' – what a lovely turn of phrase. Cawdrey's dictionary, subtitled '...for the benefit of ladies, gentlewomen, or any other unskillfull persons...' contained some 2,500 words, including both 'condiscende' and 'patronise'. The only surviving copy of *A Table Alphabeticall* is kept in the Bodleian Library in Oxford, but it was republished in 2007 under the title *The First English Dictionary 1604*. Amongst its definitions are:

■ ABRICOT, *kind of fruit* [note the French spelling] ■ FEMALE, *the she in mankind, or other* ■ MANIACQUE, *mad: braine sick* ■ ZODIACK, *a circle in the heauen, wherein be placed the signes, and in which the Sunne is mooued*

Such was the extent of the detail to be found in the dictionaries of the time, which is why Johnson's dictionary, published 149 years later, took the literary world by storm. Johnson, working alone but for the occasional clerk he hired to transcribe his chosen excerpts from books, took nine years to complete his dictionary, but the result was indisputably the most comprehensive and illustrative dictionary of its kind.

Johnson was the first to use literary quotations to support his explanations, but he rejected the term 'definition', stating in his preface:

> *'As nothing can be proved but by supposing something intuitively known, and evident without proof, so nothing can be defined but by the use of words too plain to admit a definition.'*

His was also what is called a 'prescriptive' dictionary – one that offers the author's opinion on certain words – as opposed to a 'descriptive' dictionary, which just describes them. Thus we can glean a bit about Dr Johnson's beliefs and wit. Take this entry, for example.

> 'EXCISE – *a hateful tax levied upon commodities and judged not by the common judges of property, but wretches hired by those to whom excise is paid.'*

Whereas Cawdrey listed just over 2,500 words in his *Table Alphabeticall*, Johnson's *Dictionary of the English Language* contained over 40,000. It had been commissioned by a consortium of printers with the aim of establishing a standard for the printed word in English, and Johnson fulfilled the brief. He updated his dictionary several times and it remained a respected reference tool a hundred years later, when work began on the mammoth project that would become *The Oxford English Dictionary*. Johnson took a practical view of his task:

> *'Language is not an abstract construction of the learned, or of dictionary makers, but is something arising out of the work, needs, ties, joys, affections, tastes, of long generations of humanity, and has its bases broad and low, close to the ground.'*

In the meantime, American schoolteacher (where do they find the time?) Noah Webster had compiled *An American Dictionary of the English Language* (1828). Webster was a staunch patriot who was keen to establish American independence, not just politically but culturally too. His aim in publishing his dictionary was to establish a standard for American English, which took many forms, varying wildly from one part of the country to another. To a large degree he succeeded. His decision to simplify what he regarded as overcomplicated English spellings established the Americanized spelling of words such as 'color' and 'center'. Of the 70,000 words that made it into his life's work, 12,000 had never appeared in another dictionary before.

Not long afterwards, the Reverend Dr Ebenezer Cobham Brewer, a Cambridge law graduate who also worked as a teacher, compiled one of the most famous variations on the dictionary theme, *Brewer's Dictionary of Phrase & Fable*. First published in 1870, Brewer's, as it is commonly known, explained the origin and significance of famous phrases, mythical and historical figures and other matters of interest, such as Roman numerals. Seventeen editions later, Brewer's remains a fount of valuable information. Did you know, for example, that 'crummy' used to have good connotations and also meant 'plump' or 'well developed', because it comes from 'crumb', the soft, fleshy part of the bread? Or that 'sideburns' used to be called 'Burnsides' after the American Federal General Ambrose Everett Burnside, who kept his facial hair trimmed in that style?

In 1901 another variation on the strict dictionary style was

published. *Chambers Twentieth Century Dictionary* took the format of the standard dictionary as approved by the conservative scholars of the day and added all manner of words that were not considered to be 'the Queen's English'. Contemporary slang, dialects and even archaic words made it into Chambers. And so it continues today. Look in Chambers if you want a definition for 'yoof' or 'boy band'.

Throughout this part of the late 19th and early 20th centuries, *The Oxford English Dictionary* was gestating. It had been conceived in 1857 by three members of the London Philological Society, Richard Chenevix Trench, Herbert Coleridge and Frederick Furnivall, who shared a belief that the English dictionaries of the time were not up to the job. In 1860 they began work on a new dictionary, with definitions based on quotations submitted by enthusiastic members of the public.

Coleridge was the first editor but was soon succeded by Furnivall after he died a year into the project. It soon became clear that they had spawned a monster. Fuelled by thousands of slips of paper submitted by their eager contributors – one of whom turned out to be an inmate at Broadmoor asylum for the criminally insane – the project grew and grew. It was 23 years after Coleridge's death before the first portion (from 'a' to 'ant') made it into print and a further 40 years before the first complete edition was published by Oxford University Press. Six editors had worked on the project and it was hailed as a masterpiece, one of the most important works in literary history. Within 20 years, it was out of date.

In 1957 Robert Burchfield was appointed to edit an updated supplement and 15 years later he delivered the first volume. It took a further 14 years to deliver the other three. By 1984, work had already begun on *The New Oxford English Dictionary Project*: the creation of an electronic version of the *OED*. This took a mere three years and brought all the supplements into one unified dictionary, which ran to 20 volumes. Today the *OED* is also available on CD-ROM and online by subscription, and contains 291,500 entries, updated every quarter with 1,000 new and revised entries. The next printed edition is scheduled for 2037.

See also BREWER; FOWLER; JOHNSON; WEBSTER.

DIPHTHONG

What a marvellous word is diphthong. It sounds distinctly onomatopoeic, doesn't it? It should describe the sound made when you twang the elastic in a Brazilian beach volleyball player's bathing trunks, but instead it is the name given to two vowel sounds pronounced within one syllable, as in the 'ai' sound in 'name'.

The word comes from the Greek *di* and *phthong*, meaning 'having two sounds'. (Isn't it a shame that we don't have the word 'phthong' at our disposal any more?) The two sounds are usually a combination of an 'i' or 'u' sound, as in 'elite' and 'flu' respectively, with one of the other vowel sounds. Try saying these words and pay attention to the exact sounds you're producing.

CROWD ❖ NAME ❖ SHOW ❖ TIGHT ❖ TOY

Now try pronouncing these sounds:

cra-ood ❖ *nay-eem* ❖ *shu-oo* ❖ *tie-eet* ❖ *taw-ee*

Pretty much the same, aren't they? Hopefully this illustrates the two vowel sounds being made. These are all examples of 'falling diphthongs', in which the less pronounced vowel sound comes second. That is, 'toy' has its emphasis on the 'taw' rather than the 'ee'. There are other falling diphthongs whereby the sound does not close to an 'i' or 'u' sound but remains centred as the sound changes. Try saying these.

CURE *cyoo-wer* ❖ FEAR *fee-yer* ❖ STARE *ste-yer*

With these diphthongs a 'w' or 'y' sound comes into play. This is also true of 'rising diphthongs', in which the less pronounced vowel sound comes first. 'Piano', for example, is a rising diphthong, and you can hear how the 'y' sound precedes the longer 'a' sound. Piano is, of course, an Italian word and Italian is riddled with rising diphthongs:

BIANCO ✻ CAMBIARE ✻ GIORNO ✻ IERI ✻ PIAZZA ✻ SIENA ✻ UOMO

This makes Italian a much easier language for classical singers, since a rising diphthong gives a longer pure vowel sound than a falling diphthong, allowing the singer to keep the airflow constant for longer.

To help emphasize the double vowel sound created by diphthongs, try your hand at some monophthongs (of one sound). Listen carefully to the sound you make in saying the following:

caught ✻ *cook* ✻ *coop* ✻ *cot* ✻ *cut* ✻ *rasp* ✻ *red* ✻ *reed* ✻ *tap* ✻ *third* ✻ *tip*

The word diphthong is sometimes used for pairs of vowels that produce a single sound, such as the 'au' in 'caught', and also for the archaic 'ae' in Caesar. These 'improper diphthongs' are actually digraphs.

BOUGHT ✻ HEAD ✻ SOUP

In the southern states of the United States, they might argue that the 'ea' of 'head' is indeed a diphthong, because they pronounce it 'hey-ud'. Similarly the monophthong 'e' of 'red' becomes 'ray-ud' and so on. In the North of England, you will hear the monophthong 'ou' of 'four' pronounced as a diphthong 'foo-wer'. The way we apply diphthongs to the vowel sounds largely defines our accent.

See also SONGS; VOWEL

DO

The word 'do' is magnificently versatile. The *OED* lists ten different meanings of the noun, but it's the verb we're interested in here. A subtle development has taken place over the last decade, with the verb 'to do' being applied in cases where other verbs once stood quite happily.

'We don't do fish.'

To anybody reading this sentence prior to the mid-1990s the meaning would have been, 'We don't sell fish.' Today, however, it could just as easily mean, 'We don't eat fish, and what's more we think fish is repulsive and morally wrong.' Somewhere along the line, somebody (possibly a scriptwriter for an American sitcom) took heed of the adage 'Why use several words where one will do?' and invented a new use for the word 'do'.

The word was already being transformed during the 1980s when the expression 'let's do lunch' became commonplace, the use of 'do' conveying that it was not only about eating lunch, but also the whole process of pressing the flesh, chewing the fat, running ideas up flagpoles, etc., that makes up a working lunch.

The sense of 'do' to convey the idea of a habitual process has been around for a long time.

'She does a lovely fish pie.' 'He can do a brilliant James Cagney.'

In theatrical circles this evolved into the use of 'do' with regard to adjectives, rather than nouns.

'Can you do happy for me, luvvie?'

But what has happened is not so much a change in the use of 'do', but 'do' causing a shift in the function of the object word, in this case 'happy', from adjective to noun. And this in return has reinforced 'do' as a word that implies a repertoire. Hence, 'I don't do fish' implies that fish – eating it, touching it, talking about it – is entirely beyond one's scope.

In this respect it could be argued that the new 'do' is a commendable development of the English language, were it not for the fact that it is impossible to use it in this way without coming across as nauseatingly supercilious. And I don't do nauseatingly supercilious.

See also Not; Noun; So.

DOWN

Another versatile word, 'down' can be a noun, a verb, an adjective or an adverb. It can be a rolling hill, a county in Northern Ireland or the fluffy underfeathers of a duck.

Its primary meaning, though, is 'from a higher to a lower position', and this has led to numerous other uses of the word.

down	**a.**	*behind, for example we're one–nil down*
down	**a.**	*emotionally depressed*
down	**a.**	*in agreement, for example I'm down with that*
down	**a.**	*mastered, for example he's got the subject down*
down	**a.**	*not functioning*
down	**a.**	*paid up front*
down	**a.**	*removed, for example two down, one to go*
down	**adv.**	*at a reduced level, for example turn it down*
down	**adv.**	*direction away from, for example down train, kicking down, down to Margate*
down	**adv.**	*from one generation to the next*
down	**n.**	*one of a sequence of 'plays' in American football*
down	**v.**	*to bring someone or something to the ground*
down	**v.**	*to eat or drink an entire quantity*

(**a** = adjective; **adv.** = adverb; **n.** = noun; **v.** = verb)

EMOTICON

Have you ever fallen out with someone over a joke you made in an e-mail, which came across as serious? For all their cleverness, e-mails and texting do not 'do' sarcasm (see Do) and yet they encourage quickfire intercourse (in the verbal communication sense, of course). The result is a tinderbox of potential offence, as individuals joust with each other over a medium that denies them the facility to support their flirtatious remarks with a nod or a wink. Enter the 'emoticon'. The word was first attributed to *The New York Times* in 1990 and is formed from the words 'emotion' and 'icon'. So an emoticon conveys the intended feeling behind any e-mail or text message by illustrating an appropriate facial expression using typographical characters.

The idea of using a punctuation mark to express emotion has been around for years, but the first use of emoticons within text is credited to Scott Fahlman, a computer scientist in Pittsburg, Pennsylvania.

In 1982 Fahlman posted a suggestion on the university message board that the symbols :-) and :-(should be used to distinguish between posts that were serious and those that were not. What began as a colon for eyes, a hyphen for a nose and brackets for a mouth, to indicate happiness or unhappiness, has developed into a range of symbols for misery, laughter, confusion, circumspection and more.

Symbol	Meaning	Symbol	Meaning
:) *or* :-)	HAPPINESS OR HUMOUR	:'-D	CRYING WITH LAUGHTER
:(*or* :-(	UNHAPPINESS	:I *or* :-I	INDIFFERENCE
;) *or* ;-)	IRONY OR CHEEK	:-/ *or* :-\	CONFUSION OR SCEPTICISM
X-(	ANGER	:-& *or* :-S	INCOHERENCE
:] *or* :-]	JOVIALITY	:@ *or* :-@	SHOCK OR SCREAMING
:[*or* :-[	GLUMNESS	:O *or* :-O	SURPRISE
:D *or* :-D	LAUGHTER	:-X	SECRECY

You have to turn your head to the side to get the picture, but it's a lot less distressing than thinking your wife  has actually run off with the milkman when she's only teasing.

Mobile phones and many message boards now provide emoticons pre-styled like the original smiley, so you don't have to type them out and you don't have to tilt your head to read them. Microsoft Word also automatically turns a colon/hyphen/bracket combination into a smiley symbol, which can be annoying when you're trying to write about emoticons for a book on words.

See also NEOLOGISM; TEXTING LANGUAGE.

ENGLISH

The Old English word 'englisc' was used to denote the 'Angelcynn', the Germanic tribes made up of Angles, Saxons and Jutes who colonized Britain in the 5th century AD. In time it came to apply to all peoples living in England, and their common language, not just the members of those specific tribes.

English evolved to become the most widely spoken language in the world (see Language), but that doesn't mean that everybody who speaks English uses the same words. Even on England's doorstep, in Wales, Scotland and Ireland, there are words used in English that would baffle an Englishman. While Scotland has handed over words like 'lassie' and 'slogan', it has also kept a few aces close to its chest:

CAMSTAIRY *fractious* ■ CLISHMACLAVERS *gossips* ■ FOZY *fat-witted*
■ GUMPLE-FOISTED *out of temper* ■ HUMGRUFFIANLY *repulsive*
■ KIPPAGE *disorder* ■ MIXTER-MAXTER *jumble* ■ RAMFEEZLED *exhausted*
■ RICKLE *load* ■ WANCHANCY *unlucky*
[source: the *Guardian*]

Lewis Carroll, eat your heart out! In Wales there is a smaller reserve of esoteric Englishisms, probably because of the prevalence of Welsh as a first language. Welsh has given the world a few choice words, including 'flannel', 'crumpet' and, surprisingly, 'penguin' (meaning 'white head', oddly enough). But you'll also hear a few words from the English-speaking population that will leave you nonplussed.

CARREG *stone* ✦ CLENNIG *a gift of money* ✦ DAP *bounce* ✦ PILM *dust*
✦ SALLY *willow* ✦ STEAM *bread bin*
[source: http://www.worldwidewords.org]

As for the Irish, we know they gave the world 'banshee', 'boycott' (although the latter came from an Englishman's name), 'blarney' and 'bog', but according to Daniel Cassidy, author of *How The Irish Invented Slang: The Secret Language Of The Crossroads*, hundreds more words in English have an Irish origin. Cassidy claims that 'abracadabra', 'boogaloo', 'booze', 'cahoots', 'cantankerous', 'highfalutin' and other words galore (from the Irish *go leór*, verified by the *OED*) are corruptions of Irish words. But if there is a connection, who's to say the influence didn't occur the other way round? Cassidy's theory would then be 'bunkum' (from the Irish *buanchumadh*, so he claims, although others say it is derived from Buncombe County in the USA). However, it's undeniable the Irish do have an English vocabulary which is very much their own.

CHISELER *child* ❉ COOLABOOLA *cool* ❉ CULCHIE *from the countryside*
❉ DINGEN *very good* ❉ FEEN *dude* ❉ GANSEY *sweater* ❉ GOMBEEN *corrupt activity* ❉ GOMEY *worthless* ❉ GURRIER *young rascal* ❉ JOUK *go*
[source: http://www.wikipedia.com]

See also AMERICANISM; LANGUAGE; SLANG.

EPONYM

An eponym is a word derived from a person's name. In many cases the attachment to a person is obvious, such as Archimedes' principle or Morse code. Indeed, there are many eponyms to be found in the field of science – Watt, Volt, Fahrenheit and Fallopian tube – and in place names – America, Columbia, Georgia and Leningrad. But the most intriguing eponyms are those such as 'Biro' and 'Hoover' (see Brand), which have been adopted into everyday speech to the point where the eponymist has almost been forgotten.

BOYCOTT Captain Charles Cunningham Boycott, army officer and land agent

DERRICK Thomas Derrick, hangman

SPOONERISM William Archibald Spooner, Church deacon and Oxford don

MESMERIZE Franz Mesmer, physician

GUILLOTINE Dr Joseph-Ignace Guillotin

JACUZZI Candido Jacuzzi

PYTHONESQUE *Monty Python's Flying Circus*, popular TV comedy show

LEOTARD Jules Léotard, acrobat

LYNCHING Charles Lynch, American planter and anti-British activist

NAMBY PAMBY Ambrose Philips – the nickname of this English poet first publicized in a book of that name by Henry Carey

PILATES Joseph Pilates, physical trainer

TEDDY BEAR Theodore Roosevelt Jr, American president

SADISM Marquis de Sade, aristocrat and writer

SAXOPHONE Adolfo Sax, musician and instrument maker

SHRAPNEL Henry S. Shrapnel, army officer and inventor of the shrapnel shell

See also BRAND; SPOONERISM.

EUPHEMISM

'Euphemisms are unpleasant truths wearing diplomatic cologne.'
Quentin Crisp (whose own name was a euphemism for Denis Charles Pratt)

A euphemism is a word or a phrase used in place of a more precise but less favourable expression. Instead of going to the toilet we take a comfort break. Politicians don't lie, they are economical with the truth. 'Beating about the bush', 'sugar-coating' and 'mincing words' are alternative expressions for speaking euphemistically, although not euphemisms themselves. Politics and political correctness have caused a plague of euphemisms to swarm into the English language. Some, like 'vertically challenged' instead of 'short' are clearly absurd, while others are more sinister. 'Collateral damage' has become the accepted term for 'the killing of innocent civilians'.

Indeed, death has a list of euphemisms all of its own, as does pregnancy. So too has the act of inducing the condition (there's one now).

DEAD

☠ *bitten the dust* ☠ *bought the farm* ☠ *cashed in his chips* ☠ *deceased* ☠ *departed* ☠ *given up the ghost* ☠ *gone to meet his Maker* ☠ *gone with God* ☠ *kicked the bucket* ☠ *no longer with us* ☠ *passed on* ☠ *popped his clogs* ☠ *pushing up the daisies* ☠ *shuffled off this mortal coil* ☠ *thrown a seven* ☠ *turned his toes up* ☠ *went online*

PREGNANCY AND SEX

eating for two ☺ expecting ☺ got a bun in the oven ☺ in the family way ☺ preggers ☺ with child ☺ coupling ☺ doing it ☺ how's your father ☺ making love ☺ making the beast with two backs ☺ nookie ☺ playing hide the sausage ☺ sleeping together

George Orwell said that 'political speech and writing are largely the defence of the indefensible', which is why euphemism plays such a big part in political language. If you're planning a career in politics and want to sprinkle more euphemisms into your speech, there are several techniques that are worth learning. A popular one is the use of litotes, which is conveying an opinion by denying its opposite.

> *'He's not without his faults.'* MEANING *'he's deeply flawed'.*

Next comes the use of bewilderingly long or foreign words.

> *'Economical with la verité.'* MEANING *'lying'.*

Then you must learn to turn nouns into adjectives to avoid labelling anybody.

> *'He has warmongering tendencies.'* MEANING *'he is a warmonger'.*

And finally, use abstract expressions for specific things.

> *'The Afghanistan situation.'* MEANING *'the war in Afghanistan'.*

Away from politics, Cockney rhyming slang has produced some useful euphemisms for some of the more offensive words in the English language, such as 'Richard the Third' and 'Berkshire Hunt' (see The C word). It doesn't always work that way round, though. 'Wife', for example, becomes 'trouble and strife', a fine example of dysphemism if ever there was one.

In essence, euphemism is a form of censorship, protecting the reader or listener from words that you don't want them to hear.

When politicians talk about 'responsible government', you know they mean 'cutbacks'. But it is also a way of getting around censorship. In *Lady Chatterley's Lover*, when D.H. Lawrence uses the terms 'Lady Jane' and 'John Thomas' for the female and male genitalia respectively, he is merely playing his part in a tradition that continues to this day.

Female ❖ Male
chamber of secrets ❖ *the bishop*
flower ❖ *crown jewels*
front bottom ❖ *meat and two veg*
holy of holies ❖ *orchestra stalls*
inner sanctum ❖ *pocket rocket*
private parts ❖ *privates*
rosebud ❖ *member*

See also POLITICAL CORRECTNESS.

EXPLETIVE

A common misconception is that an expletive is a swear word. In fact, it is any word that appears in a sentence without adding anything to its meaning. The Latin verb *explere*, from which it is derived, means 'to fill'. Some expletives are innocent little words like 'it' and 'there'. Look at these sentences:

> *'It is necessary to remove your undergarments.'*
> *'There are flowers in the garden.'*

In the first sentence, ask yourself what the 'it' refers to? What is necessary? Answer: the removal of your undergarments. Therefore, you could say, 'The removal of your undergarments is necessary,' and the sentence, though somewhat pompous, would be just as clearly understood without the 'it'. In the second example, you could do away with 'there' and say, 'Flowers are in the garden.'

The more obvious form of expletive, however, is the emotive word, often a profanity, that is inserted into a sentence; not to add meaning but to add feeling.

> *'The stupid television's broken.'*

The Watergate tapes contained numerous mentions of the word 'goddamned', which was considered indecent at the time and was deleted from transcripts. In their place came 'expletive deleted', the poetry of which caught on as a catchphrase which is still popular today.

See also PROFANITY.

THE F WORD

Somehow less offensive than the C word, yet more versatile and still the subject of a fair degree of censorship, the F word is assumed to be of Anglo-Saxon derivation, although its etymology is uncertain. What we do know is that it is not an acronym for Felonious Use of Carnal Knowledge or any similar expression.

There is written evidence of it dating back more than 500 years and it was successfully causing extreme offence right up to 1972, when the *OED* listed it for the first time. It was first uttered on British television by theatre critic Kenneth Tynan in 1965, but it was still taboo 11 years later when the Sex Pistols subjected interviewer Bill Grundy to a volley of F words on prime time television in the UK. Although it has been used repeatedly in films as diverse as *Four Weddings and a Funeral* and *8 Mile*, efforts are still being made to protect children from overexposure to what was once considered the rudest word of all. To that end, a number of euphemisms have been devised, but they fool nobody.

fark ☆ freak ☆ feck ☆ frick ☆ flip ☆ fudge ☆ fook ☆ fug

See also THE C WORD; EXPLETIVE; FOUR-LETTER WORDS; PROFANITY

FAMOUS LAST WORDS

So what words will you choose to utter with your dying breath? Ouch? Ho hum? Hypenemious? Or will you, like so many of the great and good, carefully construct something meaningful with which to leave your eternal mark upon the planet?

Famous last words don't have to be the very last utterances before death. It must be hard to come up with something poignant in such circumstances. Without having been there, it's impossible to say for certain that all these famous last words are genuine, but it's nice to think they are. The trick, though, is not to save your best lines until last.

'Am I dying or is this my birthday?'
Nancy, Viscountess Astor

✳

'Friends, applaud, the comedy is finished.'
Ludwig van Beethoven

✳

'I am about to, or I am going to, die; either expression is used.'
Dominique Bouhours, French grammarian

✳

'Now I shall go to sleep. Goodnight.'
Lord Byron

✳

'Goodnight, my darlings, I'll see you tomorrow.'
Noël Coward

'The earth is suffocating... Swear to make them cut me open, so that I won't be buried alive.'
Frédéric Chopin

✳

'I'm bored with it all.'
Sir Winston Churchill

✳

'Damn it! Don't you dare ask God to help me.'
Joan Crawford

✳

'It is very beautiful over there.'
Thomas Alva Edison

✳

'Bugger Bognor!'
George V, King of England

✳

'I see black light.'
Victor Hugo

'I know you have come to kill me. Shoot, coward, you are only going to kill a man.'
Ernesto 'Che' Guevara

✳

'Is it the Fourth?'
Thomas Jefferson (it was)

✳

'Does nobody understand?'
James Joyce

✳

'Why not? Yeah. Beautiful.'
Timothy Leary, writer and hippy

✳

'Why do you weep. Did you think I was immortal?'
Louis XIV, King of France

✳

'Too late for fruit, too soon for flowers.'
Walter de la Mare

✳

'I am just going outside and I may be some time.'
Captain Lawrence Oates, polar explorer

✳

'Lord, help my poor soul.'
Edgar Allan Poe

✳

'Put out the light.'
Theodore Roosevelt

'Nothing matters. Nothing matters.'
Louis B. Mayer, film producer

✳

'Go on, get out – last words are for fools who haven't said enough.'
Karl Marx

✳

'Dying is easy, comedy is hard.'
George Bernard Shaw

✳

'Dying is a very dull and dreary affair. And my advice to you is to have nothing whatever to do with it.'
William Somerset Maugham

✳

'I've had eighteen straight whiskies, I think that's the record.'
Dylan Thomas

✳

'God bless... God damn.'
James Thurber

✳

'Go away. I'm all right.'
H.G. Wells

✳

'Don't let it end like this. Tell them I said something.'
Pancho Villa, revolutionary

FECK

Now there's a word that seems to have found a loophole in our sensibilities. One vowel out but serving pretty much the same purpose as the F word, this Irish interjection has gained entry into the cocktail party of popular entertainment and stands thumbing its nose at the F word from behind the glass.

Feck, you see, doesn't mean the same thing. It has nothing to do with copulation, unless you're talking about particularly vigorous or efficient copulation; feck in English means effectiveness, value or vigour – hence feckless.

But the Irish use of the word has no such excuse because it is merely a corruption of the F word. It is used in the same way, as an expression of annoyance, but without the sexual connotation.

The Irish comedy series Father Ted made full use of this loophole, with 'feck!' 'fecker!' 'fecking!', 'feck off!' and 'feck it!' liberally sprinkled throughout the script.

See also THE F WORD.

FECUND

A lovely word, derived from the Latin *fecundus*, meaning fertile or fruitful. It appears here as momentary light relief from all the profanities. Now, where were we...?

FOUR-LETTER WORDS

'Love is just a four-letter word'
Bob Dylan

'Four-letter word' is a euphemism for 'profanity', hence Bob Dylan's double entendre. Have you ever wondered why so many profanities have four letters? Here are 16 for a start. Test your vocabulary by filling in the blanks.

F U _ _ ▶ _ U N _ ▶ _ I S _ ▶ _ H _ T
_ W A _ ▶ _ U _ D ▶ _ O _ K ▶ D I _ _
D _ R _ ▶ W _ N _ ▶ T _ T _ ▶ K _ _ B
C L _ _ ▶ _ R S _ ▶ F _ R _ ▶ T _ _ S

How many did you get?

The number of four-letter profanities is out of proportion to the rest of the English language. Four-letter words are relatively few. Most of them are of Anglo-Saxon origin and are what lexicologists now call lexemes; in other words, uninflected stems from which other words can be formed.

For example, the lexeme 'bold' gives 'boldly', 'bolder', etc., so you can see at once that this process is likely to produce many longer words. This is well illustrated by Dylan's 'love', a lexeme that yields many more words of 5, 6, 7, 8, 9, 10, 11 and even 12 letters.

❹ *Love* ❺ *Loves* • *Lover* • *Loved* ❻ *Lovers* • *Loving* • *Unlove* • *Lovely*
❼ *Beloved* • *Unloved* • *Loveful* • *Lovable* • *Lovably*
❽ *Unloving* • *Loveless* • *Lovingly* • *Unlovely* ❾ *Unbeloved* • *Loverless*
• *Belovedly* • *Unlovable* ❿ *Unlovingly* • *Loveliness* • *Lovingness*
⓫ *Lovableness* ⓬ *Lovelessness*

This shows why four-letter words are relatively few – but why so many four-letter profanities? Probably because we tend not to choose anything complex when we swear, preferring something nasty, brutal and short.

See also The C word; Expletive; The F word; Inflexion; Profanity

FOWLER, HENRY WATSON (1858-1933)

An English schoolmaster and journalist, Henry Watson Fowler wrote one of the most revered guides to the correct use of words and grammar, *A Dictionary of Modern English Usage*, known today simply as Fowler's. Together with his younger brother, Francis George Fowler, he began work on the book towards the end of the First World War, but Francis died of tuberculosis in 1918, leaving Henry to finish the project alone. *A Dictionary of Modern English Usage* was first published by Oxford University Press (OUP) in 1926 and was an instant hit amongst those scholars of the English language who wanted a definitive style guide. It was reprinted in June, August and October of that same year. In the touching dedication to his brother with which Henry introduces the book, his own erudite grip on English usage is plain to see:

'I think of it as it should have been, with its prolixities docked, its dullnesses enlivened, its fads eliminated, its truths multiplied. He had a nimbler wit, a better sense of proportion, and a more open mind, than his twelve-year-older partner; and it is a matter of regret that we had not, at a certain point, arranged our undertakings otherwise than we did...'

A second edition was published in 1965, renamed *Fowler's Modern English Usage*, and in 1996 Robert Burchfield, editor of *The Oxford English Dictionary* from 1957 to 1986, produced a third edition, heavily revised and noted for its swing from the hard and fast style of Fowler to a more permissive guide to English usage.

Fowler set out to bring modern English into line, by laying down rules that everyone could follow, and while the style he prescribed in 1926 has become outdated in some cases – you'll notice he puts a comma before 'and' in the second sentence of his introduction, something that many modern writers consider unnecessary – he provided a reference point that has helped English users ever since to avoid the pitfalls of 'not talking proper'. That said, you need a fairly proficient grasp of the English language to understand what Fowler's saying in many of his explanations. Here he is in the first edition, summing up on the subject of commas with 'and':

> 'The only rule that will obviate such uncertainties is that after every item, including the last unless a heavier stop is needed for independent reasons, the comma should be used (Every man, woman, and child, was killed; They killed every man, woman, and child.).'

After completing *A Dictionary of Modern English Usage*, Fowler helped out on the first edition of *The Shorter Oxford English Dictionary*, published in 1933. He compiled the entries under U, X, Y and Z.

See also DICTIONARY.

FREE

Always catches your eye, doesn't it?

FUDDY-DUDDY

A term of unknown origin, often used to describe an old stick-in-the-mud, someone averse to change, for example authors of books that rail against the changing use of words in the English language.

Ironically, fuddy-duddy is a relatively recent word, the first known mention dating from the start of the 20th century. 'Fuddy' could have originated as a portmanteau of 'fussy' and 'faddy', both of which bear similar meanings. The use of the word 'dud' as a useless or worthless thing came about at around the same time, so 'duddy' may be an extension of that. It was also a Scottish slang term meaning 'ragged', but this bears no relation to the meaning of fuddy-duddy.

See also PEDANT.

In the 21st century word games abound on television and radio, in newspapers and magazines and in boxed versions. However, evidence of our interest in playing with words dates back to AD1, because a word square was discovered in the ruins of Pompeii. Carved in stone, it was made up of five words, reading forwards, backwards, up and down like this.

R O T A S
O P E R A
T E N E T
A R E P O
S A T O R

HA_GMA_

Known as the Sator Square, its meaning is uncertain, yet it became a popular device. It was believed to have mystical powers and was inscribed above doorways to ward off evil. Word squares like this developed and grew over the centuries and were a popular form of puzzle in the 19th century. Also from that period we have the first records of hangman being played.

THE CROSSWORD PUZZLE

It was the memory of playing with word squares that inspired Arthur Wynne to invent the crossword in 1913. Wynne was a Liverpudlian journalist working for an American publication called the *New York World*. He was asked to create a new puzzle for the fun page and came up with a variation

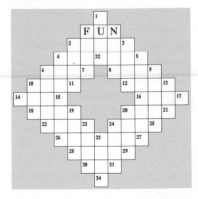

on the magic square in the shape of a diamond. Putting in just one word, 'fun', he wrote clues to the missing words and called it a word- cross – it scored an instant hit with readers. Here's Wynne's original word-cross, published in *New York World* on 21 December, 1913.

[clues]	
2-3 *What bargain hunters enjoy.*	33-34 *An aromatic plant.*
6-22 *What we all should be.*	28-29 *To elude.*
4-5 *A written acknowledgment.*	N-8 *A fist.*
4-26 *A day dream.*	30-31 *The plural of is.*
6-7 *Such and nothing more.*	24-31 *To agree with.*
2-11 *A talon.*	8-9 *To cultivate.*
10-11 *A bird.*	3-12 *Part of a ship.*
19-28 *A pigeon.*	12-13 *A bar of wood or iron.*
14-15 *Opposed to less.*	20-29 *One.*
F-7 *Part of your head.*	16-17 *What artists learn to do.*
18-19 *What this puzzle is.*	5-27 *Exchanging.*
23-30 *A river in Russia.*	20-21 *Fastened.*
22-23 *An animal of prey.*	9-25 *To sink in mud.*
1-32 *To govern.*	24-25 *Found on the seashore.*
26-27 *The close of a day.*	13-21 *A boy.*
	10-18 *The fibre of the gomuti palm*

Wynne played around with different shapes and sizes for the grid before settling on a square. By 1930, when *The Times* newspaper published its first crossword, the square grid was a familiar sight in just about every newspaper in the United States, the *New York Times* being the notable exception, and was catching on around the world. In Britain the crossword took on an extremely fiendish new dimension: the cryptic clue. The trend was set by a compiler called E. Powys Mathers, whose crosswords appeared in the *Observer* under

the pseudonym 'Torquemada'.

A number of conventions apply to cryptic crosswords. 'Out', or some other rearranging word such as 'muddle' or 'disturbed', signifies an anagram; 'heard' signifies a word or letters that sound like a word in the clue; numbers often signify Roman numerals – 'six' probably means there's a 'vi' in the answer; other clues are given by chemical symbols and other abbreviations – 'gold' signifies an 'au', silver an 'ag' and 'engineers' signifies an 're', short for Royal Engineers. These conventions were largely established in the 1940s by Torquemada's successors, 'Ximenes' (D.S. Macnutt) and 'Afrit' (A.F. Ritchie) who compiled for *The Listener*.

But it's *The Times* crossword, which leans heavily on literary knowledge as well as cryptology, that provides the most popular daily test for puzzlers on the 7.03 to London Bridge, and in 1970 the newspaper staged its first Crossword Championship. Twenty thousand people entered and it was won by a diplomat called Roy Dean.

In 1982 a crossword was compiled by Robert Turcot in Quebec, Canada, which consisted of 12,489 across clues and 13,125 down clues. It remains the largest crossword compiled to date.

In 1938 an American architect by the splendid name of Alfred Mosher Butts created a board game, laid out on a 15 x 15 grid, that was based on Wynne's original Word-Cross concept. Each player was given a set of letters from which they had to make words that interlocked on the grid. Butts called it Criss-Crosswords, but we know it today as Scrabble.

That name was the idea of James Brunot, who bought the rights from Butts in 1948 and successfully marketed Scrabble for the first time, thanks in no small part to Macy's in New York agreeing to stock the game. Since then, more than 100 million Scrabble sets have been sold in 29 different languages. It is the world's most popular word game, with its own World Championship and its own book of official Scrabble words.

Word search

In 1968, another splendidly named American, Norman E. Gibat of Oklahoma, published the first Word Search. Another game involving words in a grid, this one gave you the words amidst a jumble of random letters and all you had to do was spot them. Less cerebral than the crossword, word search puzzle books are hugely popular amongst the elderly and people looking to kill time on long journeys.

Given the mass popularity of these word puzzles, it was inevitable that they would make it on to television in some shape or form. Although the crossword has yet to be successfully adapted for the small screen, Scrabble made it on to NBC in America in the 1980s and 1990s, and many other shows, such as Britain's *Countdown*, have been based on a variation on the theme. It was the first programme to be aired by Channel 4, which began in 1982; more than 50 series later it is still going strong.

Balderdash

In 1965 another word-based gameshow launched on NBC. It was called *Call My Bluff* and the game involved two teams of three contestants trying to guess the true definition of obscure words, while their opponents tried to lead them astray with false definitions. It was short-lived in the United States, but was picked up by the BBC in Britain, where it ran from 1965 until 1988 and was brought back in 1996.

In 1984 the concept was turned into a board game by Londoners

Laura Robinson and Paul Toyne. They called it *Balderdash* and it sold in great volume. In 2004 it was turned into a gameshow for United States television, albeit briefly.

According to the *OED*, the word 'balderdash' dates back to the 16th century, when it meant a frothy liquid. It was then applied to any 'jumbled mixture of liquors', both as a noun and a verb (to balderdash), and by the end of the 17th century it had come to mean 'a senseless jumble of words or nonsense', as it does today.

Word association

A longer-running gameshow format was *Family Feud*. Launched in the United States in 1976, it was exported to the UK three years later and ran until 2002 under the less confrontational title *Family Fortunes*. It was a themed word association game that pitted families against each other – contestants had to guess the most popular words a sample survey group had come up with under a given heading. For example, if the heading was 'Christmas', the survey might list 'stocking', 'cake', 'pudding', 'gifts' and 'reindeer' in that order. If the contestant said 'stocking' they would get maximum points. If they said 'Santa', they would get no points. A similar concept lay behind *Outburst*, a board game designed by Brian Hersch in 1986. Billed as 'the game of verbal explosions', players worked against the clock to shout out all the words printed on a card under a given category.

Both games were more rigid in their format than the original word association game, whereby players just said the first word that came into their head in response to what the previous player had said. This has become a popular way to pass the time of day on Internet forums.

I could mention many more word games, but these are the best known. These game formats have helped to sell millions of newspapers, puzzle books, dictionaries, thesauruses and board games and have filled many hours of TV air time. They have also played a large part in improving the vocabulary and general knowledge of generations.

GENDER

You may remember this word from foreign language lessons at school: what gender is the noun – masculine or feminine? Some languages, such as German and English, have three genders – masculine, feminine and neuter – while others, such as French and Italian, have only masculine and feminine. In English the only evidence of gender comes in the form of pronouns: he, she or it; him, her or it; his, hers or its.

Because the genders in language are largely connected to the sex of the object in question, the word 'gender' has come to be used instead of 'sex' when distinguishing between male and female. This is wrong, according to Henry Fowler, who wrote in his *Dictionary of Modern English Usage*:

> *'To talk of persons or creatures of the masculine or feminine gender, meaning of the male or female sex, is either a jocularity (permissible or not according to context) or a blunder.'*

Gender, he stated, 'is a grammatical term only'. Nevertheless, the word has come into use as a euphemism for 'sex' on forms and surveys. Perhaps this is because so many respondents have answered 'Yes please' or 'Occasionally' when faced with the question 'Sex?'.

We get the word 'gender' from the old French *gendre*, modern form genre, meaning 'type' or 'kind'. This in turn comes from the Latin *genus*, from which we get 'generate', 'generation', etc. In the 14th and 15th centuries, it was all to do with production, be it heat, light or offspring. As a verb it could mean to copulate and to give birth; as a noun it meant a class or type, as in the Latin *genus*. Somewhere along the line this versatile word became solely a grammatical term, according to

Fowler, but in the latter half of the 20th century it found a new use amongst writers exploring the sexual divide. It has developed from there to form expressions such as 'gender-bender', meaning somebody who assumes the appearance and/or characteristics of the opposite sex.

GERUND

When a verb fulfils the function of a noun it is called a gerund. In English, all gerunds end in 'ing', the same as the present participle. But there is a subtle difference between the function of a present participle and a gerund.

'Diana likes dancing.'

'Dancing' is a gerund because it functions as the object of the sentence.

'Diana is dancing beautifully.'

'Dancing' forms part of the verb 'is dancing' and, therefore, is not a gerund.

GET

Maligned amongst English teachers, who try to encourage their students to use more descriptive words, such as 'catch', 'receive', 'consume', 'understand' or any of the many other words for which 'get' is a substitute.

The thing is that its basic meaning, to obtain or procure, can apply to any noun you want it to, from comprehension (get the joke), to faith (get religion), to virus (get the measles).

It's debatable whether or not it shows greater imagination to say 'I caught the measles' rather than 'I got the measles', but the meaning of 'get' is being twisted these days for use in situations where it sounds vulgar and greedy, symptomatic of modern times.

In *Garfield the Movie*, the hero – an embodiment of selfishness, greed and vulgarity if ever there was one (although funny too, it must be said) – pulls a stunt whereby he steals milk from a neighbour's doorstep and, by way of a convoluted, Heath-Robinson piece of cunning, consumes the lot. Wiping the residue from his whiskers, he belches and proclaims triumphantly, 'Got milk!' He speaks for all of his kind.

A similarly twisted use of 'get' that's becoming more and more common is when ordering food.

> *'Can I get a cheese and pickle sandwich?'*

Probably. How should I know? This question takes the person providing the sandwich out of the equation and suggests that you'll be fetching it yourself, as opposed to 'Can I have...' or better still, 'May I have...' or even 'Can you give me...', all of which acknowledge that there is some dependency on the provider to co-operate with the request. In short, it's polite.

Politeness is about subtlety and there is a subtle difference between getting and being given. Getting suggests that you're doing the action yourself, for example 'get the car', 'get the beers in'. So it's not the way to go about asking someone else to serve you a cheese and pickle sandwich.

GHOTI – PRONOUNCED 'FISH'

No, this is not some surrealist word game, it is an illustration, attributed to George Bernard Shaw, of the ambiguity of English spelling.

HERE'S HOW IT WORKS:

In the word 'enough', the 'gh' is pronounced 'f'.
In the word 'women', the 'o' is pronounced 'i'.
In the word 'nation', the 'ti' is pronounced 'sh'.
So, 'gh-o-ti' is pronounced 'f-i-sh'.

Thus, 'potato' could be spelt 'ghoughbteighpteau' (hiccough, though, debt, neighbour, ptomaine, bureau). Ptomaine is a substance formed in rotting organic matter, which gives a foul smell or taste.

See also PRONUNCIATION; SILENT LETTERS.

GO

Few words demonstrate the evolution of language as comprehensively as the word 'go'. Having come into English from German, with the meaning of movement from one place to another on foot, it now has dozens of meanings, including to say ('And she goes, like, whatever.') and to copulate ('Your wife – does she go?'). Let's try and trace its evolutionary path. Could it be something like this?

MOVEMENT FROM A TO B ON FOOT ⟫ *Go home.*
MOVEMENT ALONG ⟫ *So the story goes* ◆ *Go with the flow.*
EXISTENCE ⟫ *Go by the name of* ◆ *Go hungry.*
TO ELAPSE, TO RUN OUT ⟫ *Time goes by* ◆ *The food's all gone.*
TO DETERIORATE ⟫ *Go off* ◆ *Go crazy* ◆ *Go to seed.*

To PASS ⟫ *What I say goes* ◆ *Anything goes.*
To APPROVE, INVEST IN ⟫ *I'll go for that* ◆ *I'll go a fiver.*
To HARMONIZE ⟫ *Do these colours go?*
GENERAL MOVEMENT, FUNCTION ⟫ *The clock's going.*
ACTION, ENDEAVOUR ⟫ *Have another go.*
SOUND ATTACHED TO ACTION ⟫ *Cows go moo* ◆ *Guns go bang.*
SPEECH ⟫ *He goes, 'How much?'*
VIGOROUS ACTION ⟫ *Go for him!*
SEXUAL ACTIVITY ⟫ *She's a goer.*

These are just a few of the meanings of 'go'. In general, it implies action away, 'come' being the antonym, although in some cases the two are interchangeable.

'It's going to rain.' ⟿ *'It's coming on to rain.'*
'This party: who's going?' ⟿ *'This party: who's coming?'*

Amazingly, 'go' does not rank among the top ten most-used words in English. In fact, it's down somewhere in the 70s.

GRAMMAR

Anything that concerns how words are formed to indicate their function in a sentence comes under the heading of 'grammar'. Grammar is there to help us make sense of what we read and write, see and hear, but it is not essential to adhere to its rules in order to be understood. For example, 'He don't talk proper,' is not grammatically correct. It should be, 'He doesn't talk properly.' And yet its meaning is unambiguous. The big debate is this: is it a threat to the English language to allow sentences like 'He don't talk proper' to go unchecked? Or is this misuse of grammar all part of the evolution of language?

See also INFLEXION

GREEK

'It's all Greek to me.'

With records tracing its use back 3,400 years, Greek is the oldest living language. An offshoot of the Indo-European language from which all Western languages are believed to derive, it evolved from the Mycenaean civilization into Classical Greek, which spread far and wide with the Greek empire.

Modern Greek is a derivation from Hellenic Greek, a dialect which became the international language for those living and travelling around the Mediterranean and later throughout the Roman empire. The New Testament was written in Hellenic Greek and this was the vehicle by which Greek came to play such an influential part in the English language. Thanks to the Greeks we have an alphabet with vowels, we write from left to right, we have grammatical rules (although not as strict as theirs) and we have thousands of words that we would otherwise have had to invent ourselves. Towards the end of the Renaissance, scholars leaned heavily on Classical Greek to enrich the vocabulary of modern languages, including English, with sophisticated-sounding words such as 'lexicon'. Moreover, they created new words by combining Greek roots.

ARISTOCRACY *aristos = best; cratein = to rule* ◆ BIOGRAPHY *bios = life; grafein = to write* ◆ COSMOPOLITAN *cosmos = world; polites = citizen* ◆ ECONOMY *oecos = house; nemein = to manage* ◆ ORTHODOX *orthos = correct; doxa = belief* ◆ PANDEMONIUM *pan = all; daemon = demon* ◆ TECHNOLOGY *techne = art; logia = study of*

Many of these Greek compounds were later adopted back into modern Greek. But the general flow has been in the other direction, and it continues today, particularly in the field of science and technology.

ASTRONAUT *astro = star; nautes = sailor* ◆ HELICOPTER *helix = spiral; pteron = wing* ◆ MACROBIOTIC *macros = long; bios = life* ◆ PSYCHEDELIA *psyche = soul; deloun = to reveal*

While Latin is used for naming species, Greek words populate the vocabulary of medicine and chemistry.

arsenic ❖ *asthma* ❖ *bacterium* ❖ *hydrogen* ❖ *leprosy* ❖ *metabolism* ❖ *oxygen* ❖ *paralysis* ❖ *pharmacology* ❖ *rheumatism* ❖ *spasm* ❖ *trauma*

Just as the Greeks bolstered their own vocabulary with suffixes that breathed new life into old roots, English uses many Greek suffixes and prefixes in creating new words.

PREFIXES
centi ✱ *giga* ✱ *hyper* ✱ *kilo* ✱ *macro* ✱ *mega* ✱ *micro* ✱ *poly*
SUFFIXES
-cracy ✱ *-logy* ✱ *-graphy*

But in addition to the compounds made up in the Renaissance and since, there are many everyday words in the English language for which we owe thanks to Greek.

angel ❖ *chaos* ❖ *church* ❖ *democracy* ❖ *devil* ❖ *ecstasy* ❖ *government* ❖ *grammar* ❖ *hippopotamus* ❖ *logic* ❖ *monarchy* ❖ *parliament* ❖ *phenomenon* ❖ *rhetoric* ❖ *sphere* ❖ *system* ❖ *telephone* ❖ *tyrant*

The negative effect of all this Greek flooding into English was that many perfectly good Anglo-Saxon words were shoved aside to make way.

See also LATIN; OLD WORDS.

HYPERBOLE

'I've told you a thousand times not to exaggerate.'

Another word derived from Greek, 'hyperbole' – usually abbreviated to 'hype' these days – refers to a situation in which words are deliberately exaggerated in order to produce an effect, but without the intention of being taken literally.

However, in politics and entertainment, the latter part of that definition has been ignored, so, for example, when we're told, 'You've never had it so good,' (Harold Macmillan) or, 'A chicken in every pot and a car in every garage,' (Herbert Hoover) we're expected to believe it.

In its more innocent guise, hyperbole has been used extensively in the English language as a tool for describing something out of the ordinary, where 'very good', for example, just won't do. In his *Dictionary of Modern English Usage*, Henry Fowler wrote this on the subject of the word 'terribly'.

'It is strange that a people with such a fondness for understatement as the British should have felt the need to keep changing the adverbs by which they hope to convince listeners of the intensity of their feelings.'

Word purists complain about hyperbole because of the way it destroys the true meaning of words. 'Terribly' is a classic example. Its true definition – 'so as to excite terror or dread' – is hardly apt when whispering to your loved one, 'Are you terribly happy, darling?' Later on you might say, 'I miss you terribly,' which is a bit more logical but casts doubt on the happiness previously alluded to. But we all know that 'terribly', like its synonyms 'frightfully' and 'dreadfully', means nothing more sinister than 'very' or 'a lot' in this context. However, in accordance with the Greek – *hyper* = 'beyond'; *ballein* = 'throw' – these words go further than any purist alternative.

Hyperbole fashion changes quite rapidly, as different words are adopted and bent to the task, or their meaning alters. 'Terribly', for example, is still used today but rarely in a positive context. You're more likely to see it followed by words such as 'ill', 'poor', 'sad' or 'cold'. Positive statements like 'terribly happy' or 'frightfully amusing' are used to parody a bygone age in which everyone in TV and cinema spoke the Queen's English with a clipped accent. Meanwhile, 'terrific', which means the same thing as 'terrible', is used as a positive expression.

A quick look at the original meaning of a number of 'hype' words shows the influence of religion, the fear of God being a common thread. Because Christianity sees God as both dreadful and wonderful, it is easy to see how the language has used these words to apply to matters such as sport, that excite us as Christianity excited our forefathers in days gone by.

POSITIVE

AMAZING *to confuse or stupefy* ♦ ASTOUNDING *to render unconscious*
♦ AWESOME *inspiring reverence and fear* ♦ BRILLIANT *brightly shining*
♦ FANTASTIC *existing in the imagination only* ♦ PHENOMENAL *of a specific nature* ♦ TERRIFIC *inspiring terror* ♦ UNBELIEVABLE *cannot be believed*

NEGATIVE

ABOMINABLE *offensive or hateful* ♦ APPALLING *rendering shock or dismay* ♦
DIABOLICAL *of the Devil* ♦ DREADFUL *exciting dread or reverence* ♦
FRIGHTFUL *causing fright or alarm* ♦ TERRIBLE *inspiring terror (as 'terrific')*

See also FOWLER.

HYPHEN

A short line that serves to join words into compounds, the hyphen is one of the few punctuation marks in English that becomes part of a word. 'Home-made' is hyphenated in the *Oxford English Dictionary*, but you will often see it as one word, 'homemade', or indeed as two, 'home made'. The rules governing the use of hyphens are not set in stone; rather they are used to avoid ambiguity in sentences like this:

'*I swam with a man-eating fish.*' ☞ Clearly the fish is a man-eater.

'*I swam with a man eating fish.*' ☞ 'Eating' could refer to I, the man or the fish.

Hyphens may or may not be used to attach a prefix to a word, such as 'ex-girlfriend', but when the word is a proper noun, a hyphen must be used, for example 'anti-American', 'pre-Ottoman'.

See also COMPOUND.

I

The first person singular pronoun, 'I' has an interesting and relatively short history. As recently as the early 19th century, the single letter 'I' was not universally used in Britain. In the Southwest they still used the Germanic ich, or in some cases, before a vowel, just the 'ch', as in 'cham' meaning 'I am'.

The North was first to use the single letter 'i', an abbreviation of 'ik', also from the German ich. Up until the 15th century Northerners used 'ik' before a vowel and 'i' before a consonant, but it was still pronounced as in 'bit' rather than 'bite'. In the 1400s, capital 'I' became the common form everywhere except the South and its sound gradually changed to the longer diphthong 'aye'.

The Germanic *ich* began as *ek*, a derivation of *eg*, from the Indo-European *ego*, which was also used in Greek and Latin.

If there's one thing guaranteed to make a grammarian's blood boil, it's the misuse of the word 'I'.

> *'He scolded my brother and I.'*

To many people, confused as they are, this sounds correct. It isn't. 'I' should only be used as the subject of a sentence. In this case it is the object and should be 'me'. There is a sense that 'my brother and I' sounds correct, whereas 'my brother and me' does not. This is because so much school time is spent tackling the misuse of 'me'.

> *'My brother and me played football.'*

Rather than learning that 'me' is the object form and 'I' the subject form, a mild panic sets in. People assume that 'me' is bad English and go about replacing it with 'I', regardless of the rules. Because of the order in which English sentences are constructed, if you want to put yourself at the end of the sentence it's most likely that you are the object rather than the subject. But check by saying the sentence without mentioning your brother or anybody else and the correct word will become obvious.

> *'Me played football.'* ✦ *'He scolded I.'*

As a final note, avoid using 'myself' instead of 'I' or 'me'. It is the coward's way out. 'Myself' is the reflexive form, which means it is for use when the first person is both the subject and the object, as in

> *'I shot myself.'* and *'I was cross with myself.'*

> *See also* CASE.

IMPORTS

English has borrowed so heavily from other languages that it could be argued that all the words in our vocabulary are imports. Most go through a process of change, either via other languages, or by anglicized spelling and pronunciation. But some imported words do their job so perfectly that we've kept them as they are, funny spellings and all (with the exception of words translated from different alphabet systems). Here is a small selection, not including types of food and animals, which would take up a book on their own.

AARDVARK	Afrikaans
ABATTOIR	French
ANGST	German
ANORAK	Inuit
APARTHEID	Afrikaans
ARIA	Italian
BARD	Gaelic
BAYONET	French
BISTRO	Russian
BLITZ	German
BONANZA	Spanish

BRAVO	Italian
BUNGALOW	Hindi
CARGO	Spanish
CASINO	Italian
CHAUFFEUR	French
CHUTZPAH	Yiddish
CONFETTI	Italian
DINGHY	Hindi
DITTO	Italian
DUNGAREE	Hindi
EMBARGO	Spanish
ENTREPRENEUR	French
ESPIONAGE	French
FIASCO	Italian

GARROTTE	French		
GEYSER	Icelandic		
GHETTO	Italian		
GLITZ	Yiddish		
GRAFFITI	Italian		
GUERILLA	Spanish		
GUNG HO	Cantonese		
HINTERLAND	German		
INCOGNITO	Italian		
JUNGLE	Hindi		
KAYAK	Inuit		
KARAOKE	Japanese	SABOTAGE	French
KETCHUP	Malay	SAGA	Icelandic
KHAKI	Urdu	SCHADENFREUDE	German
KINDERGARTEN	German	SCHMALTZ	Yiddish
KOWTOW	Mandarin	SHAMPOO	Hindi
LOOFAH	Arabic	SHERBET	Arabic
MAELSTROM	Dutch	SIESTA	Spanish
MAESTRO	Italian	SKI	Norwegian
MANIFESTO	Italian	SOFA	Arabic
MUESLI	Swiss German	SMORGASBORD	Swedish
PAJAMAS	Urdu	STILETTO	Italian
PANACHE	French	STUDIO	Italian
PATIO	Spanish	THUG	Hindi
PENGUIN	Welsh	TORNADO	Spanish
PROPAGANDA	Italian	TREK	Afrikaans
PUKKA	Hindi	TSUNAMI	Japanese
PUNDIT	Hindi	TYCOON	Japanese
REGATTA	Italian	TYPHOON	Mandarin
RENDEZVOUS	French	VENDETTA	Italian
ROBOT	Czech	WOK	Cantonese
SAUNA	Finnish	YOGHURT	Turkish

INFLEXION

Also spelt 'inflection' and derived from the Latin *inflectere*, to bend, inflexion, when applied to words, is the modification of a word to indicate gender, person, tense, etc. The basic, uninflected form of the word is called a 'lexeme'. For example, 'write' is a lexeme and its inflexions include:

writes ✳ writing ✳ wrote ✳ written

'Writer', however, is not an inflexion but a derivation, since it is not a form of the verb 'to write' but a noun formed from the lexeme 'write'. In strict terminology, the standardized form of a lexeme is called a lemma, and this is what you see as the headword for each entry. Derivations like 'writer' are also classed as lemmas and will have their own entry.

INSULT

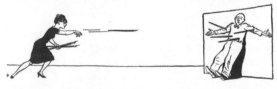

'Sticks and stones may break my bones But words will never hurt me.'

Yeah, right. The contention that words will never hurt has been challenged ceaselessly throughout the history of mankind and with great skill in many cases. Brought into English via French, from the Latin *insultare* (to leap in), the origins of 'insult' suggest an attack without warning. Insults come in two forms: name-calling and wit. The two are mutually exclusive. Name-calling changes with fashion: you're unlikely to be called a 'cad' or a 'bounder' these days, just as a Victorian would not have shouted 'loser!' or 'muppet!' at a rival. Wit, on the other hand, survives the passage of time.

'*I find the ass in compound with the major part of your syllables.*'
William Shakespeare (*Coriolanus*)

＊

'*Fine words; I wonder where you stole them.*'
Jonathan Swift

＊

'*I didn't attend the funeral, but I sent a nice letter saying I approved of it.*'
Mark Twain

＊

'*If all the girls who attended the Yale prom were laid end to end, I wouldn't be a bit surprised.*'
Dorothy Parker

＊

'*I never forget a face, but in your case I'll be glad to make an exception.*'
Groucho Marx

Bessie Braddock: '*Winston, you are drunk!*'
Winston Churchill: '*Bessie, you are ugly, but tomorrow morning I shall be sober.*'

Lady Astor: '*Winston, if you were my husband I would flavour your coffee with poison.*'
Winston Churchill: '*Madam, if I were your husband I should drink it.*'

Telegram from George Bernard Shaw: '*I am enclosing two tickets to the first night of my new play, bring a friend – if you have one.*'
Telegram from Winston Churchill: '*Cannot possibly attend first night, will attend second – if there is one.*'

Some of the best insults, however, have been in response to provocation. Winston Churchill seemed to stir other people into insulting him, but usually managed to hit back with a winner.

But you have to go a long way to find a wittier insult than Margot Asquith, wife of the British Prime Minister, uttered to Hollywood's platinum sex bomb Jean Harlow. Tired of Harlow pronouncing the 't' at the end of Margot, she eventually snapped back, 'No Jean, the "t" is silent, as in Harlow.'

JARGON

Jargon is an old French word for the chattering of birds: it is also used to describe any unintelligible talk. Its modern use applies to speech or writing that is heavily laden with esoteric words that are understood only by the members of a particular group.

This is nothing new. Sailors and soldiers have for centuries had their own jargon: 'port', 'starboard', 'abaft', 'landlubber', 'mizzen'; 'civvy', 'dingbat', whizz-bang'. Slang, and Cockney rhyming slang in particular, is a form of jargon, understood only by those in the know.

While the hi-tech world constructs its jargon with new words ('botnet', 'dongle') and politics and business build theirs on unlikely combinations ('whip', 'balloon mortgage'), the legal profession leans heavily on Latin ('sub judice', 'habeas corpus') and other foreign languages ('tort', 'voir dire'), as well as words that fell out of common usage centuries ago ('hereinafter', 'heretofore'). Lawyers will argue that this 'legalese' is actually a vocabulary of technical terms, but the purpose remains the same: to make what you say so impenetrable that nobody outside the profession dares to question it.

See also BUZZ WORD; CLICHÉ; COMPUTER LANGUAGE.

JOHNSON, DR SAMUEL (1709–1784)

'Leaving already, Doctor? Not staying for your pendigestatery interludicule?'
Edmund Blackadder to Dr Johnson in the *Blackadder* episode 'Ink and Incapability', written by Richard Curtis and Ben Elton

Samuel Johnson was an 18th century English writer who single-handedly wrote *A Dictionary of the* *English Language* over a period of ten years. Containing 42,773 words, this was the first dictionary compiled with the aim of including every word in the English language, together with explanations and quotations.

Johnson came from a poor family in Lichfield, in the English Midlands, but his father's profession – bookseller – stood him in good stead. Though he surrendered a place at Oxford University because he couldn't afford the fees, he began a writing career that would see him become one of the most influential literary figures of his, and indeed any, age.

Single-mindedness, knowledge, resourcefulness, pride and wit were the attributes that enabled Johnson to forge a prominent literary career from unprivileged beginnings, and all are evident in the story of how he compiled his dictionary. Embarking on what he thought would be a three-year project, he secured funding to the tune of 1,500 guineas and sought to augment this figure by appealing to London's aristocracy for patronage, among them Lord Chesterfield, from whom he received nothing of any significance. Undaunted, he stuck to the task alone, eventually finishing the work after ten years. Advance reviews hailed the dictionary as a masterpiece, including one by Lord Chesterfield in which he claimed to be patron of the project.

Piqued by this, Johnson wrote a damning letter to Chesterfield, scorning the notion of patronage, which he made public by publishing it in the dictionary's preface. It included the sentence, *'Is not a patron, My Lord, one who looks with unconcern on a man struggling for life in the water and when he has reached ground encumbers him with help?'*

This sent shockwaves through London society and, some say, helped to break the metaphorical chains that shackled writers to their patrons. Johnson did, however, accept a pension from the king in later life, which ensured that he no longer endured poverty he had known when young. He was buried in Westminster Abbey.

See also DICTIONARY.

JOKES

'Humour is the first of the gifts to perish in a foreign tongue.'
Virginia Woolf

How and why mankind came to invent words  remains uncertain, but there's a fair chance that it was done to provide an alternative to the visual gag. Charlie Chaplin would have done well before the birth of language, but most comedians depend on the clever use of words for their humour. In many cases it is the words themselves that are the joke.

The old 'my dog's got no nose' joke is funny because of the way the verb 'to smell' is both transitive and intransitive in English. However, the joke works in any language where this is the case:

> *'Je dis, je dis, je dis... Mon chien n'a pas de nez.'*
> *'Ton chien n'a pas de nez? Comment-il sent?'*
> *'Mauvais!'*

But, as Virginia Woolf so rightly pointed out, most wordplay gets lost in translation.

> **Q:** *Do you have vertigo?* **A:** *Only as far as the bus stop.*

This would be lost on the French, for whom 'vertigo' (*vertige*) sounds nothing like 'far to go' (*loin aller*).

Similarly, there are wordplay jokes that only work when spoken:

> **PATIENT:** *'Doctor, Doctor, one minute I think I'm a wigwam, the next minute I think I'm a teepee.'* **DOCTOR:** *'You're too tense.'*

But wordplay goes way beyond the corny pun. There's a catalogue of jokes based on Spoonerisms, such as:

> **Q:** *What's the difference between a market trader and a sausage dog?*
> **A:** *One balls out his wares...*

The word 'joke' entered the English vocabulary in the late 17th century, as a variation of the Italian *gioco* from the Latin *jocus*, meaning a jest. It was a late arrival for a phenomenon that had been around for thousands of years. The oldest joke ever told is not recorded – although the finger points at Bruce Forsyth – but it is safe to assume that it closely followed the first word ever uttered. Jokes and wordplay were rife amongst the ancient civilizations, and the fact that some of Shakespeare's humour is still funny today shows that the things that make us laugh remain fairly constant.

KN WORDS

Words beginning with awkward double consonants used to be common in Old English, for example *cneo* (knee), *cniht* (knight), *hlud* (loud), *hrof* (roof), *hwil* (while). These letters were all pronounced, but over time it became easier to drop the initial consonant and the spellings gradually changed accordingly. Not, though, in the case of the 'cn' words, which later adopted the German and Dutch 'kn' form. This is possibly because there are several cases where dropping the 'k' would leave a word with a very different meaning.

KNOW ♦♦♦ NOW	KNIGHT ♦♦♦ NIGHT	KNELL ♦♦♦ NELL
KNAVE ♦♦♦ NAVE	KNEW ♦♦♦ NEW	KNEE ♦♦♦ NEE
KNOT ♦♦♦ NOT	KNAP ♦♦♦ NAP	KNIT ♦♦♦ NIT

See also SILENT LETTERS.

LANGUAGE

It is thought that all Western languages have descended from one ancient language known as Indo-European. This is a theoretical language only because there is no written form of it, but evidence of its existence comes from words used by its descendant languages, which include Sanskrit, Greek, Latin, Persian, Gothic (Germanic) and Celtic.

As the Indo-European civilization spread from its homeland and broke up, its language evolved into distinct forms, including Sumerian, whose cuneiform inscriptions on clay tablets are amongst the earliest known forms of the written word, dating back some 5,000 years.

The highly structured Sanskrit language has remained intact for 2,000 years and it was this that provided the initial evidence of one ancient language that encompassed the area that ran from Europe into the Indian subcontinent. The theory was put forward in 1786 by a British scholar called Sir William Jones, who noted the structural similarities between Sanskrit, Greek and Latin. Further study revealed so many similarities between words that the theory became indisputable.

While the Indo-European family was evolving out of eastern Europe and western Asia, the Semitic language family was spreading into the Arabian peninsula, possibly from East Africa, and spawning Arabic – the language of Islam – and Hebrew among others.

The English language evolved from the Germanic branch of the Indo-European family, with heavy influence from the Greek, Celtic and Italic. Today English is the first language of about 310 million people, second only to Mandarin, but its popularity as a second language has made it the predominant global language, with the total number of English speakers worldwide approaching two billion. It is the official international language of aviation and shipping, as well as an official language of the United Nations and the European Union.

The spread of English around the world dates back to the early 17th century, when the first British colony was established in America. The expansion of the British Empire took the language to Africa, Asia and Australasia, and imposed it on the colonized population. Today there are more fluent English speakers in India and China than anywhere else on earth, but history suggests that this will not always be the case.

LATIN

The language of Latium, which spread across Western Europe with the Roman Empire, left a lasting legacy in the modern Romance languages of French, Spanish, Portuguese, Italian and Romanian, not to mention the alphabet that is used by more of the world's population than any other writing system. After the Roman Empire, Latin lived on as the language of the Roman Catholic Church and, being the common language of Europe's educated classes, was the adopted language of science and the law. English, though originally a Germanic language, owes more than half of its vocabulary to Latin, although most of these words entered the language via French and the other Romance languages.

That Latin, dismissed by some as a 'dead language', is still taught in English schools today shows its value as a template for modern languages. It lives on in the language of law and science and is widely used in the mottos of organizations as diverse as schools and the military. Also, although we might not realize it, we all use Latin every day in abbreviations.

AD *anno domini* ✱ **AM** *ante meridiem* ✱ **EG** *exempli gratia* ✱ **NB** *nota bene* ✱ **PA** *per annum* ✱ **PM** *post meridiem* ✱ **PS** *post scriptum* ✱ **QED** *quod erat demonstrandum* ✱ **RIP** *requiescat in pace*

SEE ALSO *English; Greek; Latin.*

LEXICOGRAPHY

A word constructed from the Greek *lexikon* (word book) and *graphein* (to write), lexicography is the practice of writing dictionaries.

LOGO

What began as a piece of marketing jargon around the 1930s is now a familiar term for the symbol representing a company or organization. It is an abbreviation of 'logogram', a word derived from the Latin logos (word) and *gram* (something written). Originally used for a word puzzle it then became a symbol representing a word and finally a form of trademark.

LONG WORDS

Good old Anglo-Saxon English didn't go in much for long words. Monosyllables were the norm until the Normans invaded England in 1066 and brought their Latin-based vocabulary with them. But the Anglo-Saxon lexicon was not wiped out, so today we have a choice of short or long words, depending on whom we want to impress.

ASK	*demand*	HOME	*residence*	TALK	*conversation*
DRINK	*beverage*	LIVE	*inhabit*	WAGE	*salary*
FIGHT	*conflict*	LOVE	*adore*	WHORE	*prostitute*

The use of long words is taken as a sign of knowledge and education, because it was the educated ruling classes that used the French- and Latin-influenced vocabulary, while the peasant classes continued to use Anglo-Saxon. There are names given to molecules that are thousands of letters long, but these don't make it into the dictionary.

The longest word to achieve that is this 45-letter mouthful:

pneumonoultramicroscopicsilicovolcanoconiosis

Constructed from Greek, its definition is given as 'a lung disease caused by the inhalation of very fine sand and ash dust'. The longest non-technical word to make it into the dictionary is:

floccinaucinihilipilification

At 29 letters, this is another made-up word, reckoned to have been invented as a joke by a student at Eton College, who found four ways to say 'I couldn't care less' in Latin – *flocci facere, nauci facere, nihili facere* and *pili facere* – put them together and added -fication at the end, to mean the action or habit of estimating as worthless.

For the longest sensible non-technical word in the *OED*, however, we come down to 28 letters with the one most people have heard of:

antidisestablishmentarianism

The word arose in the 19th century to describe opposition to the proposed disestablishment of the Church of England. Some of the world's more lyrical languages, like Welsh and Maori, have contributed place names that run to dozens of letters.

Llanfairpwllgwyngyllgogerychwyrndrobwllllantysiliogogogoch

This village on Anglesey is famous for having the longest name in Britain. It means, 'St Mary's church in the hollow of the white hazel near to the rapid whirlpool and the church of St Tysilio of the red cave'. But a mere 58 letters, it can't hold a candle to the 85 letters of New Zealand's

Taumatawhakatangihangakoauauotamateaturipukakapikimaungahoronukupokaiwhenuakitanatahu

LYRICS

The word 'lyric' stems from the Greek *lura* or lyre, a stringed instrument, and originally referred to poems that were intended to be sung. 'Lyric' then became the term for any short, sentimental poem. However, 'lyrics' are now mainly seen as being the words to popular music.

Libretto

An Italian word meaning 'little book', 'libretto' has entered the English language as an operatic term for the words to a musical composition.

While English, with its vocabulary of long and short words, seems to work best for the lyrics (see Lyrics) of modern music, Italian is better suited to opera because of its pure, rounded vowel sounds. Try singing the word 'piano' like an Italian ('pyarno') and then sing it again as an English singer would. You'll notice that the flow of air from your lungs is impeded when you sing in the English way whereas the Italian way enables you to make a fuller, stronger sound on the 'a' vowel. All the falling diphthongs in English have a similarly debilitating effect, which is why, if you ask an opera singer to sing the words 'how now brown cow', they'll sing it something like this:

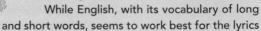

'ha-u na-u bra-un ca-u'

See also DIPHTHONG; SONGS; VOWEL.

MALAPROPISM

An eponym derived from Mrs Malaprop, a character in *The Rivals*, written by R.B. Sheridan in 1775, who habitually got her words muddled up to comical effect. Sheridan took the name from the word 'malapropos', which was in use at the time to mean inappropriate, a compound of the French expression *mal à propos*. From this we still have 'à propos', or 'apropos', meaning 'with regard to'.

Malapropism is the misuse of words, usually where one word is mistaken for another, and it is nature's way of punishing people who try to impress with fancy language with which they are not entirely er... funicular. Here's Mrs Malaprop at her best.

> *'He is the very pineapple of politeness!'* (pinnacle)
> *'Oh! it gives me the hydrostatics to such a degree.'* (hysterics)
> *'...she's as headstrong as an allegory on the banks of Nile.'* (alligator)
> *'...he can tell you the perpendiculars.'* (particulars)

Common malapropisms include 'irregardless' instead of 'regardless' or 'irrespective', 'comprising of' instead of 'comprising' or 'consisting of' or even 'comprised of', and 'laxadaisical', an unintentional portmanteau of 'lax' and 'lackadaisical'. Here are some modern-day Malaprops who will never live it down.

> *'We shall reach greater and greater platitudes of achievement.'* (plateaux)
> Allan Lamport, former Mayor of Toronto
> *'I might just fade into Bolivian...'* (oblivion)
> Mike Tyson, boxer
> *'Well, that was a cliff-dweller.'* (cliff-hanger)
> Wes Westrum, baseball star

See also BUSHISMS UNDER AMERICANISM; EPONYM.

One of a very few words in the English language to begin 'mn', mnemonic comes from the Greek *mnemos* (mindful) and means 'pertaining to memory'. More specifically, a mnemonic is a series of words – usually a saying or poem – that serve as an aid to memory. For example, 'Never eat Shredded Wheat' is a popular mnemonic for the four cardinal points, NESW. This is a fairly straightforward mnemonic because North, East, South and West are instantly recognizable from their initial letters alone. Similar mnemonics apply in music:

'GOOD DAY AUNTY EDITH' *strings on a violin:* **GDAE**
'ALL COWS EAT GRASS' *notes between lines on the bass clef:* **ACEG**

Some mnemonics, though, still require a modicum of decoding, for example where the first letter of each word corresponds to the first letters of the sequence you want to remember, but not the actual words:

'RICHARD OF YORK GAVE BATTLE IN VAIN' *colours of the rainbow:*
red, orange, yellow, green, blue, indigo, violet

In mathematics, the mnemonics become more complicated still. In this example you have to count the number of letters in each word:

'HOW I WANT A DRINK, ALCOHOLIC OF COURSE, AFTER THE HEAVY CHAPTERS INVOLVING QUANTUM MECHANICS' *pi to 14 decimal places:* **3.14159265358979**

The key to a successful mnemonic is to condense it to a memorable word or phrase. The last example stretches this somewhat.

See also ACRONYM.

MORSE CODE

'What hath God wrought'

Samuel Finley Breese Morse was a man of many talents and proof that science and art do mix. Born in Charlestown, Massachussetts, in 1791, Morse earned a reputation as a painter. He attended the Royal Academy in London and travelled around Europe developing his skills. On the voyage home across the Atlantic, he was introduced to the concept of electromagnetism and quickly turned his attention to the task of developing an electrical telegraph.

After spending several years on the project he convinced the United States Government to invest in his invention. On 24 May 1844 he sent his first official telegraph message between Washington and Baltimore. Being a religious man, the words he sent were, 'What hath God wrought.' There were other electric telegraph systems being developed at the time, but the success of Morse's invention lay in the code he created with the assistance of Alfred Vail, which enabled words and numbers to be transmitted by way of an electrical current down a wire.

The code comprised an arrangement of dots, dashes and pauses, each letter and number being represented by a different combination of dots and dashes. Morse and Vail took care to give the most commonly used letters the shortest codes. The important thing was that it could be quickly deciphered by a trained receiver.

A . _	N _ .	1 . _ _ _ _	H	U . . _	8 _ _ _ . .
B _ . . .	O _ _ _	2 . . _ _ _	I . .	V . . . _	9 _ _ _ _ .
C _ . _ .	P . _ _ .	3 . . . _ _	J . _ _ _	W . _ _	0 _ _ _ _ _
D _ . .	Q _ _ . _	4 . . . . _	K _ . _	X _ . . _	
E .	R . _ .	5	L . _ . .	Y _ . _ _	
F . . _ .	S . . .	6 _	M _ _	Z _ _ . .	
G _ _ .	T _	7 _ _ . . .			

The beauty of Morse code was that it was adaptable for just about any medium. As radio came in, the clicking dots and dashes that had initially been punched out on a tape became sonic 'dits' and 'dahs'. Morse code could also be transmitted by switching lights on and off and we've all seen the films where an SOS signal is sent by hitting a spanner against the hull of a ship: three dots, three dashes, three dots.

Contrary to popular belief, SOS does not stand for Save Our Souls; it doesn't even stand for the letters SOS. The famous distress signal was a German invention adopted by the International Radiotelegraphic Convention in 1908. Because three dots is the code for S and three dashes the code for O, SOS became a way of remembering the distress signal code. Skilled telegraphers are reckoned to be able to receive Morse code at a rate approaching 100 words per minute, although the official record stands at 75.2 wpm, set way back in 1939. Sending the code with a straight key is a little slower, the current record standing at 35 wpm.

MUPPET

Originally a puppet created for television by Jim Henson in the 1970s, 'muppet' has made it into the *Oxford English Dictionary* as a derogatory term for a naïve or stupid person.

See also INSULT; NAÏVE.

MURRAY, JAMES AUGUSTUS HENRY (1837–1915)

James Augustus Henry Murray was the first paid editor of *The Oxford English Dictionary*. He took charge of the project in 1879 but died in 1915, 13 years before the first edition was published.

See also DICTIONARY.

NAÏVE

One thing that gives the learner of English an advantage is its lack of accents. French has its acutes, graves, circumflexes and cedillas, Spanish has its tildes, German its umlauts and so on. English does away with accents, except in the case of the occasional imported word like 'café' or 'éclair', which can be written with or without the accent. The exception that proves the rule – 'prove' in this expression meaning 'test', as in 'proving ground' and 'the proof of the pudding' – is 'naïve', which is one of the few words in English to be written with a diaeresis mark (like an umlaut) on the 'i'. Diaeresis, from the Greek *diaerein* (to divide), is the division of a double vowel into two syllables. Once upon a time it indicated the correct pronunciation of words like noöne and coöperate but, possibly to simplify the typewriter keyboard, it was often replaced with a hyphen or split into two words (no one, co-operate). Naïve, however, was not composed of separate parts like 'no one', but was a whole word derived from the Latin *nativus* (of birth). It could not be split in two with a hyphen, and so the diaeresis mark remained. Bowing to the fashion of the times, the *OED* has now dropped this and lists the word as simply 'naive', although it also lists the original French spelling *naïf* and *naïveté* as versions of the noun. It would be nice to think that the loss of the diaeresis mark will not result in the pronunciation changing over time to 'nave', but perhaps that's naïve.

NAMES

The names we give our children are among the most important words we ever use, even though many of us are unaware of their meaning when we go through that tortuous process of choosing the right one. In most cases it's the sound of the name or, more significantly, the people we associate with it that sways our decision. For example, how many parents who called their daughter Emily – the most popular

girl's name in the United States every year since 1996 –
were influenced by the fact that it is derived from a Latin
word meaning 'rival'? By the same token, Adolf suffered a
marked fall in popularity after the Second World War. But delve into the
etymology of names and you find that these single words often stand for
a whole sentence. It's a shame that we don't continue this practice and
give our children names according to how we'd like them to turn out.
Then we could be rubbing shoulders with people called Fifteenminute-
celebrity, Dotcommillionaire and Taxdodger. Here is a list of the top 20
most popular boys' and girls' names in the UK in 2007, with meanings.

GIRLS

1 GRACE *grace* **2** RUBY *the precious stone* **3** OLIVIA *invented by Shakespeare in* Twelfth Night **4** EMILY *from Latin aemulus, meaning 'rival'* **5** JESSICA *invented by Shakespeare in* The Merchant of Venice **6** SOPHIE *French form of Greek Sophia, meaning 'wisdom'* **7** CHLOE *Greek meaning 'green shoot'* **8** LILY *the flower* **9** ELLA *component of longer names, from Germanic alia meaning 'other'* **10** AMELIA *from Germanic amal, meaning 'work'*

BOYS

1 JACK *form of John, originally from Hebrew meaning 'God is gracious'* **2** THOMAS *Greek form of Aramaic Te'oma, meaning 'twin'* **3** OLIVER *either 'olive tree' or form of Germanic Alfihar, meaning 'elf army'* **4** JOSHUA *from Hebrew Yehoshu'a, meaning 'God is salvation'* **5** HARRY *form of Henry, from Germanic heimiric, meaning 'home ruler'* **6** CHARLIE *pet form of Charles, from Germanic ceorl, meaning 'man'* **7** DANIEL *from Hebrew Daniyyel, meaning 'God is my judge'* **8** WILLIAM *from Germanic Wilhelm, meaning 'desire protection'* **9** JAMES *from Latin form of Jacob, meaning 'supplanter'* **10** ALFIE *from Old English aelf raed, meaning 'elf counsel'*

Source: Office For National Statistics (UK)

See also DICTIONARY.

NEOLOGISM

If you've read this book in page order, you'll have already deduced the meaning of 'neologism' from the Greek *neo* (new) and *logos* (word). A 'neologism' is just that, a new word, and it's the nemesis of any lexicographer who, like Samuel Johnson or Noah Webster, sets out to encapsulate every word in the language in one publication.

Neologisms have always been a feature of the English language. Shakespeare was a master at creating new words and new uses for old ones, and 'neologism' was itself a neologism around the end of the 18th century, a product of the fashion for creating new words from Greek compounds. Literature has always been a rich source of neologisms but in the modern era it has been overtaken by technology, with business and popular culture not far behind.

For a word to enter the dictionary it must stay in use for a reasonable length of time and be quoted by several sources. A look at the Internet (a late 20th century neologism) reveals thousands of neologisms that may or may not survive to earn a place in a major dictionary. Most won't. *The Oxford English Dictionary* contains over 300,000 main entries with an average of 600 added each year.

Those that do catch on are the words that are instantly meaningful and easy to understand; words that fill a hole in our vocabulary or enable us to express things quicker than we could before. This is why business jargon is a fertile (perhaps overfertile) source of neologisms.

Neologisms come from a variety of sources. One is what Lewis  Carroll termed a 'portmanteau' word, combining and contracting two words into one, for example 'motel', a blend of 'motor' and 'hotel'. Another is the functional shift in use, for example a noun being used as a verb, as in 'to benchmark'.

Abbreviations and acronyms can turn into words in their own right, for example 'fan' (from 'fanatic') and 'laser' (Light Amplification by the Stimulated Emission of Radiation). Sometimes a foreign word, such as *chuddies* (Hindi for underpants) enters the vernacular and street slang is always good for a regular supply of neologisms, such as the onomatopoeic 'bling'.

Rarer are words that are formed from a phrase, such as 'jobsworth', a petty bureaucrat who refuses to bend any rules on the grounds that 'It's more than my job's worth.' 'Jobsworth' could be classed as a portmanteau word, but it requires more than the two words that form it to explain its origin. Here are some recent neologisms:

PORTMANTEAU

AFFLUENZA *affluence influenza* ✱ EUROCRAT *European bureaucrat* ✱ METROSEXUAL *metropolitan heterosexual* ✱ NETIQUETTE *net (Internet) etiquette* ✱ PODCAST *iPod broadcast* ✱ PREQUEL *previous sequel*

FUNCTIONAL SWITCH

ASK *verb to noun* ✦ TASK *noun to verb*

ABBREVIATIONS AND ACRONYMS

E-MAIL *electronic mail* ✱ NEWBIE *newcomer*

EPONYMS

BUSHISM *George W. Bush* ✦ HENMANIA *Tim Henman*

IMPORTED

FATWAH *Arabic* ✱ GLASNOST *Russian*

STREET SLANG

BLING *onomatopoeia* ✦ BRITNEYS *rhyming slang*

See also ABBREVIATION; ACRONYM; EPONYM; IMPORTS; PORTMANTEAU; SLANG

NO

A tiny word that speaks volumes, 'no' can be a noun ('so that's a no then?'), a verb ('he's got to yes or no it sooner or later'), an adjective ('there's no point in going on') and an adverb ('it's no better than it was before'). The truly interesting thing about the word 'no' is the way it springs to our lips as an exclamation of negative emotion, or perhaps a denial of the fact.

Someone pushes you out of a window – 'NO!' *fear*
The opposition score a goal – 'NO!' *disappointment*
You check your bank balance – 'NO!' *shock*
You find you've been burgled – 'NO!' *dismay*
You stub your toe – 'NO!' *pain*

More often than not, when we don't have time to think of something really profane, it's the innocent little 'no' that comes out first.

See also YES.

NONCE

Nonce is English prison slang for a sex offender, more specifically a child abuser, but this has nothing to do with nonce words, which are words that were coined for use on one particular occasion and not expected to be used again. The term 'nonce word' was created by James Murray, editor of the *OED*, from the archaic expression 'for the nonce', which means 'for this one occasion only'.

An often-cited example of a nonce word is 'quark', which was used by James Joyce in *Finnegan's Wake* as a word for the cry of a seabird. It's one of many neologisms that characterize the book and, as onomatopoeia goes, it was a good invention. However, rather than becoming an established word for the cry of a seabird, 'quark' resurfaced in physics as the name of a type of elementary particle. Physicist Murray Gell-Mann changed the pronunciation to rhyme with 'pork'. The *OED* now lists over 3,100 nonce words, most of which have lived up to their name; which makes it a little odd that they made it into the dictionary in the first place, since a nonce word is really just a neologism that hasn't caught on.

NOT

'What a totally amazing, excellent discovery. NOT!'
Wayne's World

It's difficult to explain the etymology of 'not' without using the word 'not': it's a cut-down form of 'nought', originally meaning 'not anything at all'. It comes from the Old English *awiht*, literally meaning 'ever a whit', which was the archaic equivalent of 'anything'. Putting the adverbial prefix 'ne' in front of it negated its meaning, giving 'naught', 'nought', 'nowt' and eventually 'not'. So the idea of a negating adverb was there before 'not' came about.

We take it for granted, but the ability to negate the sense of any word or phrase simply by adding one short word is one of the great faculties of language.

> IT'S GOOD. *It's not good.* ■ I'M GOING TO THE PICTURES. *I'm not going to the pictures.* ■ DO YOU LIKE CHEESE? *Not much.*

And, of course, we often make the word shorter still by apostrophizing it, as in 'wasn't', 'isn't', etc. The 1992 film *Wayne's World*, starring Mike Myers and Dana Carvey, gave us a new way of using 'not'. You just say the opposite of what you really think and then add an emphatic 'NOT!' at the end, preferably after a short pause.

NOUN

A noun is the grammatical term for a word or group of words designating a person, place or thing. Nouns fall into two main categories: proper nouns and common nouns. Proper nouns are the names of unique entities, such as people, places and organizations, and begin with a capital letter in English, for example 'Trevor', 'Swindon' and the 'Roman Empire'. Common nouns are the words for generic things or concepts and do not take a capital letter, for example 'humour', 'nose' and 'ice cream'. Both can be animate or inanimate.

Furthermore, nouns are divided into 'concrete' and 'abstract'. A concrete noun is something that physically exists, for example 'woman', 'hat' and 'purse'. An abstract noun is a state, emotion, quality, etc., that

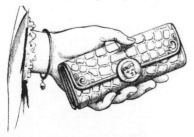

does not have physical form, for example 'poverty', 'hope' and 'pointlessness'.

If you're feeling energetic you can divide nouns further into 'countable' and 'uncountable' nouns. You can probably guess the distinction. Countable nouns can be singular or plural, uncountable are singular only, for example 'rain', 'dirt' and 'joy'. These are not to be confused with 'collective' nouns, which are singular nouns that refer to groups, for example

'company', 'army' and 'team'. Grammatically, these can be treated as singular or plural. For example 'the team is playing well' or 'the team are playing well'. It's a matter of style.

Nouns can be formed from verbs (see Gerund):

♦ *winning* ♦ *losing* ♦ *writing*

And from adjectives:

♦ *the meek* ♦ *the lonely* ♦ *the poor*

They can be compounds of verbs and adjectives:

♦ *fly-past* ♦ *take-over* ♦ *warm-up*

They can even be whole phrases:

♦ *changing of the guard* ♦ *man about town* ♦ *fly in the ointment*

Any word or phrase that performs the function of a noun is called a 'substantive'.

Sometimes it works the other way and a noun will function as an adjective:

♦ PEARL DIVER *'pearl' tells us about the 'diver'* ♦ FOOTBALL PITCH *'football' tells us about the 'pitch'* ♦ CLIFF PATH *'cliff' tells us about the 'path'*

Or as a verb:

♦ STONEWALL *to block or resist* ♦ HIGHLIGHT *to bring to attention* ♦ GREEN-LIGHT *to give the go-ahead*

See also ADJECTIVE; ADVERB; VERB.

NUMPTY

One of the more recent insults to enter the English language, 'numpty' serves the purpose of denigrating a person as stupid without alluding to race, sex, or physical handicap. It is a word for the modern age.

OBNOXIOUS

Good word, obnoxious. But the meaning we attribute to it today – offensive, objectionable – is practically the opposite of its original meaning in English, which was 'subject or liable to harm'. So it's gone from describing the victim to describing the culprit. Both are valid in accordance with its Latin origins. The 'noxious' part comes from *noxa*, meaning 'harm', while the *ob* bit was a Latin prefix that could either mean 'towards, in the way of' or 'against, in opposition to'. Hence 'obverse' (the opposite). Somewhere along the line, round about the middle of the 17th century, the understanding of 'liable to harm' changed from meaning 'liable to suffer harm' to 'liable to cause harm'.

Words themselves can be obnoxious. Insults and profanities are, of course, but some words that are not intended to offend turn out to be obnoxious because of what they imply. 'Talent', for example. This word has many meanings, from an ancient unit of weight and currency to a disrespectful term for the women of a given area. But it is also a word used in entertainment to distinguish the performers and writers from everybody else. As if a cameraman has no talent. It is also Australian slang for 'frequenters of the underworld', which is probably more appropriate.

'Creative' is another one, for similar reasons. A word coined in advertising circles to mean the copywriters and designers, not only is it making a noun out of an adjective, which is a sure sign of a dodgy buzz word, it also implies that all the other jobs are done by uncreative automatons. Some accountants are highly creative.

See also INSULT; MUPPET; NEOLOGISM.

OF

'I should of listened harder in English and then I would of understood.'

One of the most commonly misused words in English, due entirely to pronunciation, 'of' has fooled countless people into believing it is the word that forms the perfect conditional tense of verbs, when, of course, it should be 'have'. The problem arises because of the way we abbreviate 'I should have' to 'I should've', which sounds more like 'I should of'. But you only have to consider the way you form other participles, such as 'I have listened' and 'I had listened', to realise that 'of' has no part to play in the formation of verbs. So leave it alone!

OK

'OK rules OK'

Before graffiti became an art, the expression 'rules OK' or 'rule OK' could be seen everywhere in Britain, usually with the name of a football team in front of it. 'United rule OK.' It was just one of the countless applications of the world's favourite word.

The most successful of all acronyms, like its synonym 'all right', OK can be used in a variety of ways, from the enthusiastic 'She's OK by me', to the lukewarm 'The food was OK.' But it is easier to say than 'all right', and easier to write, so it has transcended language barriers and become a multilingual expression.

There are many theories as to its origin: a native American word; a corruption of the Scottish 'och aye' (oh yes); a derivation from the French *au quai* (to the quay – supposedly to do with the clearance of goods). But most evidence points to an American expression of the early 1830s, 'oll korrect', as a jokey misspelling of 'all correct'. This was picked up by the Democrat Party for the 1840 election and used as a buzz word for their candidate, Martin Van Buren, whose nickname was 'Old Kinderhook', after the name of his hometown. Four decades later, on 26 October 1881, a 30-second shoot-out took place between cowboys and law officers in Tombstone, Arizona. The gunfight at the OK Corral became the most infamous shoot-out in Wild West history.

Sometimes spelt as a lower case 'o.k.', or even written out 'okay', OK has spawned offshoots such as 'okey-doke' and, thanks to Ned Flanders in *The Simpsons*, 'okily-dokily'.

OLD WORDS

Just as language is constantly expanding, so too do words constantly fall out of use. Words that your granny used are met with bewilderment by their great-grandchildren: 'wireless', 'besom', 'beau'. But don't give up on them. Like clothes and music, words have a habit of coming back into fashion.

Here's a list of old words that are ripe for a comeback:

ALABANDICAL *barbarously drunk* ✻ BLATERATION *babbling chatter* ✻ CACATORY *attended with looseness of the bowels* ✻ COQUINATE *to behave as a cook* ✻ EGROTE *to feign illness* ✻ FALLACILOQUENCE *deceitful speech* ✻ FOPPOTEE *a simpleton* ✻ HYPENEMIOUS *full of wind* ✻ INGORDIGIOUS *greedy* ✻ JOBLER *one who does small pieces of work* ✻ MISQUEME *to offend* ✻ PIGRITUDE *laziness* ✻ RURICOLOUS *living in the country* ✻ SLIMIKIN *small and slender* ✻ TORTILOQUY *crooked speech* ✻ VENIALIA *minor offences*

See also NEOLOGISM.

It's funny how the smallest words often have the most meanings. 'On' is a prime example. From its original meaning of 'in contact with' it has evolved to serve a multitude of subtly different purposes. Other words could well be used for most of them but in many cases 'on' is the easier option. In fact, you could almost write an entire book on 'on' and all of its uses, but let's try not to bang on:

Sense • *Example*

ABOARD
- *'Get on the bus.'*

ACCEPTABILITY
- *'That's just not on.'*

ACCORD
- *'All right, you're on.'*

AGAINST
- *'They practised one on one.'*
- *'Don't be so hard on yourself.'*

AHEAD
- *'Will this be relevant 50 years on?'*

AROUND
- *'The earth spins on its axis.'* • *'The shockwaves centred on San Francisco.'*

AS A BASIS
- *'Variations on a theme.'*
- *'Congratulations on your wedding.'*
- *'You've lured me here on false pretences.'*
- *'I'm relying on you.'*
- *'Is this a horse worth betting on?'*
- *'This is a book on words.'*

ATTACHMENT
- *'The dog's on a lead.'*
- *'Whose side are you on?'*

ATTENDING TO
- *'She was on her guard.'*
- *'They were on their best behaviour.'*

- 'Put two big bouncers on the door.'
- 'The player on the ball.'
- 'He's still on his main course.'
- 'Keep your mind on the game.'

COMPARISON
- 'Year on year.'

CONSUMING
- 'Are you on drugs?'
- 'The tractor runs on pig manure.'

EARNING
- 'They're on 50 pounds an hour.'

FROM
- 'We must draw on all our resources.'

INCLUSION
- 'She's on the committee.'
- 'What's on the menu?'

IN CONTACT WITH (USUALLY ABOVE)
- 'The cat stood on the mat' (but not always).
- 'There's gum on the sole of my shoe.'

IN OPERATION
- 'The kettle's on.'

LOCATION
- 'We live on the river.'
- 'The gallery is on Trafalgar Square.'
- 'The play opened on Broadway.'

ODDS IN FAVOUR
- 'The favourite was 3 to 1 on.'

PLAYING
- 'Mick Jones on guitar.'

POSSESSION
- 'He's got a gun on him.'
- 'He's got a temper on him.'

PROGRESSING
- 'The army is on the march.'
- 'This milk's on the turn.'
- 'The workers are on strike.'
- 'The show must go on.'
- 'Is the dinner on?'

RISK
- 'On pain of death.'

• *'On the off chance.'*

SUPERIORITY

• *'She's got 15 years on him.'*

SUPPORTED BY

• *'Stand on your own two feet.'*

TIME

• *'It'll be all right on the night.'*

• *'On hearing the news.'*

TOWARDS

• *'The soldiers fired on the fortress.'*

• *'Napoleon marched on Moscow.'*

• *'A swarm of locusts descended on the fields.'*

• *'The teacher turned her eye on Johnny.'*

• *'She's keen on him.'*

• *'The joke's on you.'*

• *'The drinks are on me.'*

• *'The trains collided head on.'*

USING

• *'It was made on a sewing machine.'*

• *'He managed to fly the plane on one engine.'*

• *'She's on the computer again.'*

• *'He's always on the phone.'*

ONE

'To forget one's purpose is the commonest form of stupidity.'
Friedrich Nietzsche

The French have a similar word on, which does the same job as 'one' in Nietzsche's statement and could well be where we got this meaning from, but the use of 'one' in this way, as an indefinite pronoun, is becoming more and more rare in English.

These days Nietzsche would probably have said, 'To forget your purpose is the commonest form of stupidity.'

'One' is regarded as rather formal or pompous in modern English, particularly when used in the first person, as in Virginia Woolf's *A*

Room of One's Own, which today would be 'A Room of My Own'.

But there is something lacking in this phasing out of 'one', because it actually implies something subtly different, something a little more general than 'my' or 'I'.

Take this sentence:

> *'He dropped the baton; one could have wept for him.'*

Yes, it could be rewritten as 'I could have wept for him,' but that gives the sentence a specifically personal angle that is not there in the first instance. 'One could have wept for him' implies that not only the speaker felt that way but that it was also the general mood. But 'they could have wept for him' doesn't do the job either, so what we tend to do is use 'you' in this instance, which is more of an anomaly, since the literal 'you', the person being told, wasn't even there. It's a classic case of taking the unsatisfactory middle ground between two unsatisfactory options and is further evidence of the pronoun being something of a rogue element in the English language.

See also THEY.

ORANGE

Not the only fruit, but perhaps the only fruit to have no rhyme. Or perhaps not. We get the word 'orange' from the Sanskrit *naranga*, itself a borrowed word although nobody is sure where it was borrowed from. With the trade in oranges around the world went the word, changing slightly as it went from Persia (*narang*) to Arabia (*naranj*) to Spain (*naranja*) to Italy (arancia) to France (*orange*).

The House of Orange-Nassau, whence came William of Orange and which remains the ruling family in the Netherlands (hence all that orange regalia), gets its name from the Roman town of Orange in the South of France. The town was a major market for the fruit and over time its name changed from the Roman Arausio to Aurenja, and later to Orange.

William I, count of Nassau (Germany), became Prince of Orange in 1544 and renamed his domain the House of Orange-Nassau. This included parts of the Netherlands, which later became the seat of the ruling house as the Dutch won independence from Spain and Orange itself returned to French rule.

Which is all very interesting, but a digression from the point, which is that there is no proper word in the English language that rhymes with orange. It's not unique in this; there are many non-rhyming words in the dictionary, but orange is such an everyday word that you would expect to find a rhyme for it. Here are a few more ordinary words that drive poets crazy:

angry ❋ else ❋ empty ❋ film ❋ luggage ❋ office ❋ pint ❋ penguin ❋ silver ❋ sixth ❋ width ❋ wolf

See also RHYME.

OXYMORON

Who could fail to love the word 'oxymoron'? Contrived from two contradictory Greek words, *oxy* (sharp) and *moros* (dull), an 'oxymoron' is a phrase that puts together two contradictory statements, deliberately for effect, for example 'A deafening hush'.

'The exception that proves the rule' is often labelled an oxymoron, because surely an exception only disproves a rule. But 'prove' in this case means 'test', a sense of the word that still exists in terms such as 'proving ground', where cars are tested.

Sometimes expressions that were not intended to be oxymorons are sardonically dubbed as such. Things like 'corporate responsibility', 'hospital food', 'friendly fire' and 'military intelligence' for example.

> *'Military intelligence is to intelligence what military music is to music.'* Groucho Marx

With people like Marx about, companies that call themselves things like Dynamic Construction and Intelligent PR are asking for it.

PALINDROME

A 'palindrome' is a word or phrase that reads the same backwards, for example 'rotor'. An early example is the word square found in Pompeii in AD79 (see Games), which is made up of the words 'sator arepo tenet opera rotas'.

One of the most famous palindromes is the one concerning Napoleon: 'Able was I ere I saw Elba', in which the word spacing is exactly mirrored. Cleverer still are palindromic phrases where the words themselves are not all palindromic, for example 'A man, a plan, a canal – Panama!'

'Rotavator' is probably the longest commonly used palindrome in the English language, but the Finns outdo that by a considerable margin with 'saippuakivikauppias', which means 'seller of soap-stone'. Not something you come out with in everyday conversation perhaps, but a valid word nonetheless.

From 'palindromes' we get the neologism 'semordnilap', which is defined as a word that forms a different word when spelt backwards. The eagle-eyed amongst you will have noticed that 'semordnilap' is 'palindromes' spelt backwards, rather than 'palindrome', so it doesn't really work. But here are some more semordnilaps:

DOG ⇗ GOD   LIVED ⇗ DEVIL   DELIVER ⇗ REVILED

PEDANT

The word 'pedant' originally meant 'teacher' but it came to be used for anyone who placed too much importance on rules or details. When it comes to words, and the use thereof, you will find pedants lurking in every corner, telling you when you should use 'whom' instead of 'who' and 'may' instead of 'might'. They act like a brake on the train that carries language forward, bridling at any grammatical error, misuse or false quotation. 'Actually, I think you'll find that should be, "All that glisters is not gold," not, "All that glitters." ' A good way to catch out a pedant is to mispronounce the word when accusing them of it. Try calling them a 'peedant' and wait for them to correct you.

See also FUDDY-DUDDY.

PHONETICS

'Phonetics' is the study of the way words are sounded, more specifically the sound (phoneme) represented by each vowel and consonant in any given word. Some beautiful-sounding words are used for the different sounds. Describing the part of the mouth where the sound is made we have:

LABIAL Using the lips
- BILABIAL for example, 'm', 'p'
- LABIO-DENTAL for example, 'v', 'f'

CORONAL Using the front of the tongue
- DENTAL for example, 'd', 'n', 't'
- ALVEOLAR for example, 'z', 's'
- POST-ALVEOLAR for example, 'ch', 'j'

DORSAL Using the mid tongue, for example 'g' (hard), 'k', 'q'
- PALATAL 'y' (as in 'you')
- VELAR for example, 'ng', 'wh'

GLOTTAL Using the glottis (space between the vocal chords)
- for example, aspirate 'h' and unsounded 't'

These are the consonants used in English. We miss out on such treats as uvular dorsal and pharyngeal radical consonants, but we have enough for our needs, especially when you break these down further according to the ways in which the sound is made. Each kind of airflow has its own descriptive term: nasal, plosive, fricative, approximant, trill and flap.

The International Phonetic Alphabet (IPA) lists all of the different vowel and consonant sounds in all of the world's languages, together with symbols. The IPA is what dictionaries use to show the correct pronunciation of words. It is regularly updated and revised to take into account changing styles of speech.

This table shows the symbols for the most common phonemes in English.

VOWELS					
ɑː	HARM	aʊ	HOW	ŋ	STINGRAY
æ	HAT	eɪ	HAY	r	RAT
e	HEAD	eə	HAIR	f	FOX
ə	HEAT<u>HER</u>	ɪə	HEAR	v	<u>V</u>OLE
ɜː	HER	əʊ	HOE	θ	PY<u>TH</u>ON
ɪ	HIT	ɔɪ	HOY	s	<u>S</u>ERPENT
iː	HE	ʊə	HEWER	z	<u>Z</u>EBRA
ɒ	HOT			ʃ	<u>SH</u>ELLFISH
ɔː	HAW	**CONSONANTS**		ʒ	PER<u>S</u>IAN
ʊ	HOOD	p	<u>P</u>IG	h	<u>H</u>OG
uː	WHO	b	<u>B</u>AT	l	<u>L</u>EMUR
ʌ	HUT	t	<u>T</u>IC	j	<u>Y</u>AK
		d	<u>D</u>OG	ʧ	<u>CH</u>AFFINCH
DIPHTHONGS		k	<u>K</u>ITE, <u>C</u>AT	ʤ	<u>J</u>AY
aɪ	HIVE	g	<u>G</u>ECKO	w	<u>W</u>EEVIL
aɪə	HIRE	m	<u>M</u>OOSE		
		n	<u>N</u>ARWHAL		

See also CONSONANT; DIPHTHONG; PRONUNCIATION; RHYME; VOWEL.

PLACE NAMES

The Romans left a surprisingly small number of place names, which suggests they were happy using the existing names of the towns they colonized.

❖ **CASTRA** (town or fort)
   DONCASTER, MANCHESTER
❖ **COLONIA** (settlement)
   LINCOLN
❖ **PORTA** (gate) SOUTHPORT
❖ **PORTUS** (harbour)
   PORTSMOUTH
❖ **STRATA** (street) STRATFORD

Nowhere is the development of the English language more graphically laid out than on a map of England. Some place names go back more than 2,000 years. Though modified a little over time, they still bear testament to the Celts, Romans, Anglo-Saxons, Vikings and Normans who created them.

The Celts were largely driven out of England but their legacy remains, particularly in the extremities furthest from mainland Europe, such as Cornwall and Cumbria.

❖ **COMBE** (deep valley)
   ILFRACOMBE, SALCOMBE
❖ **PEN** (hill) PENRITH, PENZANCE
❖ **POL** (pool) POLPERRO,
   POLZEATH
❖ **TRE** (farmstead) TREVOSE,
   TREBARWITH

It was the Anglo-Saxons who really put their language on the map. To begin with they kept things simple, combining the name of the settler with the word 'ingas', meaning 'the people of'. This was abbreviated to 'ing'. They then added two very familiar elements:

❖ **HAM** homestead
❖ **TUN** or **TON** farmstead

And as their settlements grew and took on more features, the place names became more elaborate:

- **BURNA** (stream) EASTBOURNE
- **DENU** (valley) WILLESDEN
- **DUN** (hill) CROYDON
- **INGHAM** (the homestead of the people of) BUCKINGHAM
- **INGTON** (the farmstead of the people of) BRIDLINGTON
- **LEAH** (clearing) ILKLEY
- **MERE** (pond) CROMER
- **STAN** (stone) HUNSTON
- **STEDE** (site of a building) HAMPSTEAD
- **WORTH** (enclosure) RICKMANSWORTH

Next came the Vikings, who did most of their naming in the Northeast of England and East Anglia.

- **BY** (farmstead or homestead) WHITBY
- **DALR** (valley) WENSLEYDALE
- **GATHR** (gate) HARROGATE
- **HOLMR** (flat ground by a river) HOLMFIRTH
- **THORPE** (outlying farmstead) CLEETHORPES
- **THVEIT** (clearing) ESTHWAITE
- **TOFT** (plot) LOWESTOFT

By the time the Normans arrived, most of the naming had been done. They went around adding their names to existing ones, giving us some of the more cumbersome-sounding locations such as Stoke Mandeville and refining some of the Germanic spellings. But happily they did nothing about the catalogue of hilarious place names to be found in Britain. Here's just a small sample:

BISHOPS ITCHINGTON ★ COCKERMOUTH ★ FINGRINGHOE ★ LICKHAM BOTTOM ★ LITTLE SNORING ★ LUSTY ★ MINGES ★ NOB END ★ PIDDLE ★ PRATT'S BOTTOM ★ RAMSBOTTOM ★ SHATTON MOOR ★ THONG ★ UPPER DICKER ★ WETWANG

See also NAMES.

POLITICAL CORRECTNESS

The late 20th century was a revolutionary era in terms of combating prejudice. Racism, sexism, classism, ageism, sizeism... forms of discrimination that had gone virtually unchecked for thousands of years were suddenly brought to book. We should be proud of that. The downside was that something of a witch-hunt took place as people eager to affirm their own sound ideology sniffed out evidence of prejudice in even the most innocent of remarks. This was political correctness gone cerebrally challenged.

As a result, political correctness is one of the most ridiculed and reviled elements of modern English, its original good intentions lost amid a fog of lily-livered euphemisms and deliberately ambiguous waffle. Nevertheless, it has left its mark, with many PC terms now being the norm in everyday English.

chairperson *the suffix 'man' is now best avoided so as not to perpetuate any assumptions that all the key jobs are held by men.*

human resources *a way of saying 'staff' or 'personnel' without the connotations of master and servant, by placing humans on a par with paper clips.*

inappropriate *used to describe bad behaviour without actually naming the fault. It is applied to everything from bad language to child molestation.*

issues *a euphemism for 'problems'.*

partner *generic term that avoids any allusion to marital status, sexuality or living arrangements.*

special *a word used to avoid saying 'disabled' or any of its other awkward synonyms, as in 'special needs'. In a BBC poll, this was actually voted the fifth most offensive expression to describe physically or mentally disabled people.*

See also EUPHEMISM.

PORTMANTEAU

A 'portmanteau' word was a term coined by Lewis Carroll for a word that combines elements of two or more words. A portmanteau is a large suitcase and Carroll's reasoning (through the character of Humpty Dumpty) was that such a word is 'two meanings packed into one word'. Portmanteau words have added greatly to the English lexicon, and not just since Carroll's time. A lot of place names are portmanteaux, combining a person's name with a word for the type of place and sometimes a natural feature. Birmingham, for example, is a portmanteau of Beormund (name), 'ingas' (the people of) and 'ham' (homestead), meaning 'homestead of the people of Beormund' (see Place names).

'Goodbye' is a portmanteau word, a blend of 'God', 'be', 'with' and 'ye', the 'with' losing out altogether. In fact, when you look at the etymology of most words they turn out to be portmanteaux, particularly those derived from Greek or Latin.

Here are some commonly used portmanteau words from the modern era:

ADVERTORIAL *advertisement and editorial* ✱ AFFLUENZA *affluence and influenza* ✱ BLOG *web and log* ✱ BREATHALYSE *breath and analyse* ✱ BRUNCH *breakfast and lunch* ✱ CAMCORDER *camera and recorder* ✱ EMOTICON *emotion and icon* ✱ GLITZ *glamour and ritz* ✱ GUESSTIMATE *guess and estimate* ✱ MOCKNEY *mock and cockney* ✱ MOOBS *man and boobs* ✱ NETIQUETTE *Internet and etiquette* ✱ OXBRIDGE *Oxford and Cambridge* ✱ SITCOM *situation and comedy* ✱ SMOG *smoke and fog* ✱ SPAM *spice and ham* ✱ TELETHON *telephone and marathon* ✱ TRAVELOGUE *travel and monologue* ✱ WORKAHOLIC *work and alcoholic*

See also CARROLL; SHAKESPEARE; NEOLOGISM.

A prefix is an element added to the beginning of a word to modify its meaning. In most cases a prefix needs the word to which it is attached to make any sense. This is the case with the prefixes we've acquired  from Greek and Latin, which were not words in their own right. Anglo-Saxon prefixes, however, are different. The prefixes they gave us were all words in their own right, so you will have no difficulty in recognizing these:

Prefix	Meaning	Gives us
A	▷ *on*	▷ aground, ashore
BY/BE	▷ *beside*	▷ bystander, bylaw
	▷ *past*	▷ before, bygone
	▷ *also for emphasis*	▷ bedraggle, bemoan
FORE/FOR	▷ *in front*	▷ forelock, forewarn
	▷ *without*	▷ forgo, forfeit
ON	▷ *on*	▷ onlooker, onset
OUT	▷ *away from*	▷ outdate, outlandish
OVER	▷ *over*	▷ overboard, overdo
UN	▷ *not*	▷ unskilled, unsure
UNDER	▷ *under*	▷ understand, undergarment
UP	▷ *up*	▷ upstanding, uphill
WITH	▷ *against or away*	▷ withstand, withdraw

These Germanic prefixes were all prepositions that were attached to other words to give new meanings. The Greeks and the Romans, on the other hand, created prefixes specifically to be attached and, as a consequence, they gave us a lot more.

The proliferation of Greek prefixes in English is largely thanks to Renaissance scholars, who made a concerted effort to augment the English vocabulary with sophisticated-sounding words and chose Greek, the language of their education, as their chief resource.

Prefix	Meaning	Gives us
AMPHI	both, of both sides, around	amphibian, amphitheatre
ANTI	against	antidote, antagonize
APO	off, from	apoplexy, apocalypse
ARCH	high, chief	architect, archangel
AUTO	self	automatic, autograph
DECA, DEC	ten	decagon, decimate
DYS	bad	dyslexia, dysentery
ECTO	outside of	ectoplasm, ectopic
ENDO	within	endocrine, endorphin
EP, EPI	upon, at, in addition	epicentre, epidermis
EU	good, well	eulogy, euphemism
HEMI	half	hemisphere
HOLO	whole	holistic, hologram
HOMO	same	homosexual, homogenous
HYPER	above, beyond	hyperspace, hyperbole
HYPO, HYP	under, less than	hypocrite, hypothesis
ISO	equal	isobar, isometric
KILO	thousand	kilogram, kilometre
MACRO	long, large	macrobiotic, macrodynamics
MEGA	great	megaton, megalomania
META, METH	between, with, after, beyond	method, metabolism
MICRO	small	microbiology, microscope
MONO	one	monoplane, monotonous

NEO	⤳ *new*	⤳ neologism, neonatal
PAN, PANTO	⤳ *all, every*	⤳ pandemic, panacea
PERI	⤳ *around, about*	⤳ periscope, peripatetic
POLY	⤳ *many*	⤳ polygon, polygamy
SYN, SYM	⤳ *together, with*	⤳ synthesis, sympathy
TELE	⤳ *far off*	⤳ television, telescope

Many Latin prefixes came into English via French. As a result, Latin doesn't seem to feature in as many English neologisms as Greek but it does make up a huge proportion of our vocabulary.

Prefix	Meaning	Gives us
AB	⤳ *away from*	⤳ abnormal, abscond
AD	⤳ *towards, near*	⤳ advocate,
AMBI	⤳ *around, both*	⤳ ambidextrous, ambivalent
ANTE	⤳ *before*	⤳ antechamber, antenatal
BI, BIS	⤳ *two*	⤳ bicycle, biscuit
CO, CON, COM	⤳ *together, with*	⤳ coagulate, conspire
CONTRA, CONTRO	⤳ *against*	⤳ contrary, controversy
DE	⤳ *down, from, away, off*	⤳ denude, debase
DIS, DIF	⤳ *apart, away, not*	⤳ disappear, disclose
E, EX	⤳ *out, beyond, from, out of*	⤳ egress, extreme
EXTRA	⤳ *beyond*	⤳ extramural, extracurricular
IN, IR, IM, IL	⤳ *not, without*	⤳ inconsistent, inefficient
IN, IM	⤳ *in, on, upon, into, towards*	⤳ invoke, impel
INTER	⤳ *between*	⤳ interact, international

INTRO	⟩⟩ within	⟩⟩ introspection, introvert
MAGNI	⟩⟩ *great*	⟩⟩ magnificent, magnitude
MAL	⟩⟩ *bad, ill*	⟩⟩ malodorous, malcontent
MILLI	⟩⟩ *thousand*	⟩⟩ millipede, millimetre
MIS	⟩⟩ *less, wrong*	⟩⟩ misinterpret, misfire
MULTI	⟩⟩ *many, much*	⟩⟩ multiply, multitude
NON, NE	⟩⟩ *not*	⟩⟩ nondescript, nonsense
OMNI	⟩⟩ *all*	⟩⟩ omnibus, omnipresent
PARA	⟩⟩ *beside, beyond*	⟩⟩ paranormal, paradise
PER	⟩⟩ *through*	⟩⟩ perpetrate, perturb
PRE	⟩⟩ *before*	⟩⟩ previous, prevent
PRO	⟩⟩ *before, forward, forth*	⟩⟩ progress, prohibit
POST	⟩⟩ *after*	⟩⟩ posthumous, postmodern
RE	⟩⟩ *again, anew, back*	⟩⟩ reclaim, revert
RETRO	⟩⟩ *back, backward, behind*	⟩⟩ retrospective, retrograde
SEMI	⟩⟩ *half*	⟩⟩ semicircle, semiquaver
SUB	⟩⟩ *under, below, up from below*	⟩⟩ submarine, substandard
SUPER	⟩⟩ *above, down, thoroughly*	⟩⟩ superfluous, superannuated
TRANS	⟩⟩ *over, across*	⟩⟩ transfer, transition
TRI	⟩⟩ *three*	⟩⟩ triangle, trivia
ULTRA	⟩⟩ *beyond*	⟩⟩ ultramarine, ultraviolet
UN	⟩⟩ *not*	⟩⟩ undecided, undo
UNI	⟩⟩ *one*	⟩⟩ uniform, unique

A prefix can also be a word that is habitually used in conjunction with another word or phrase. In England, for example, it's actually very hard to get a cup of tea. It has to be 'a nice cup of tea'.

See also GREEK; LATIN; SUFFIX.

PREPOSITION

*'This is the kind of offensive impertinence up with which
I will not put.'*

One of the oldest 'rules' in grammar is that you should never end a sentence with a preposition. One of the oldest jokes when addressing this 'rule' is to deliberately choose a preposition to end your second sentence with. There, that's that taken care of. The common prepositions in English, in case you would like to follow this 'rule', are:

---

aboard ✻ *about* ✻ *above* ✻ *across* ✻ *after* ✻ *against* ✻ *along* ✻ *amid*
✻ *among* ✻ *around* ✻ *as* ✻ *at* ✻ *before* ✻ *behind* ✻ *below* ✻ *beneath*
✻ *beside* ✻ *besides* ✻ *between* ✻ *beyond* ✻ *but* ✻ *by* ✻ *concerning*
✻ *considering* ✻ *despite* ✻ *down* ✻ *during* ✻ *except* ✻ *excepting*
✻ *excluding* ✻ *following* ✻ *for* ✻ *from* ✻ *in* ✻ *inside* ✻ *into* ✻ *like*
✻ *minus* ✻ *near* ✻ *of* ✻ *off* ✻ *on* ✻ *onto* ✻ *opposite* ✻ *outside* ✻ *over*
✻ *past* ✻ *plus* ✻ *regarding* ✻ *round* ✻ *save* ✻ *since* ✻ *than* ✻ *through*
✻ *to* ✻ *towards* ✻ *under* ✻ *underneath* ✻ *unlike* ✻ *until* ✻ *up*
✻ *versus* ✻ *via* ✻ *with* ✻ *within* ✻ *without*

The tortured efforts of grammatical pedants to avoid ending sentences with prepositions gave rise to the famous quotation at the top of the page, which is generally attributed to Winston Churchill. It was a comment scribbled on a government document in reply to a note from a civil servant, who had pointed out a sentence ending with a preposition. Whoever was responsible did a good job of highlighting just how absurd the 'rule' can get.

It is now generally accepted that there is nothing wrong with ending a sentence with a preposition, unless it happens to be a superfluous preposition, as in this sentence.

'Where are you going to?'

The 'to' is surplus to requirements but don't worry, you don't have to say, 'To where are you going?' or even 'Whither are you going?' 'Where are you going?' is enough. The same applies to sentences like, 'Where's the sheriff at?' There's no need for the 'at'.

While we're talking about superfluous prepositions, 'off of' is another common example, especially in the United States. 'Get off of your horse and put your hands in the air.'

One instance where a 'double' preposition is called for is 'into'. Actually, 'into' is a single word preposition, but it's made up of two others and should not be substituted by in alone. 'He walked in the house,' means he was already in the house and walked around within it. You have to use 'into' in this instance.

PROFANITY

'At no time is freedom of speech more precious than when a man hits his thumb with a hammer.'
Marshall Lumsden, journalist

Generally used as a posh alternative to a 'swear word', a profanity is any act or word that is unholy or blasphemous. The word comes from the Latin *pro* (before) and *fane* (temple). What is interesting is the innate human tendency to respond to sudden pain by deliberately spouting words we know will shock or cause offence. A lot of words exist for the sake of avoiding profanities: 'heck' and 'hey' for 'Hell'; 'gosh', 'golly', 'gawd' for 'God'; 'gee', 'jupiter', 'jiminy' for 'Jesus'; 'dash', 'darn', 'dang' for 'damn'. 'Bloody' is the subject of debate. There's a theory that this is a contraction of 'by our lady', referring to Mary. 'Bloody hell', so the theory goes, means 'by our lady in Hell'.

See also THE C WORD; EXPLETIVE; THE F WORD; FOUR-LETTER WORDS

PRONUNCIATION

One of the features of the English language that makes it so lovable is its utterly inconsistent rules on pronunciation. Where Germanic and Romance languages collide there is bound to be some turbulence. This poem illustrates the problem for those trying to learn the language.

HINTS ON PRONUNCIATION FOR FOREIGNERS

by 'T.S.W' (some say George Bernard Shaw)

'I take it you already know
Of tough and bough and cough
and dough?
Others may stumble, but not you,
On hiccough, thorough, lough
and through.
Well done! And now you
wish perhaps
To learn of less familiar traps?

✳

Beware of heard, a dreadful word,
That looks like beard and sounds
like bird.
And dead: it's said like bed, not bead

✳

For goodness sake don't
call it "deed"!
Watch out for meat and great
and threat,
(they rhyme with suite and

straight and debt).

✳

A moth is not a moth in mother,
Nor both in bother, broth in brother.
And here is not a match for there,
Nor dear and fear for bear and pear,
And then there's dose and
rose and lose –
Just look them up – and goose
and choose,
And cork and work and card
and ward.
And font and front and word
and sword,
And do and go and thwart and cart

✳

Come, come, I've hardly made a start!

✳

A dreadful language? Man alive,
I'd mastered it when I was five!'

See also PHONETICS.

PROPAGANDA

'If you tell a lie big enough and keep repeating it, people will eventually come to believe it.'
Joseph Goebbels

Propaganda is a deliberate, aggressive manipulation of words to create a predetermined reaction amongst its listeners. A key trick is to avoid specifics, allowing the listeners to fill in their own interpretation of the words. A good example is the word 'they', which leaves each listener to fill in their own idea of who 'they' are. And, as Goebbels repeatedly pointed out, repetition is essential.

In 1937 a group of journalists and social scientists in America formed the Institute for Propaganda Analysis, with the aim of educating the American people in the recognition of propaganda. They drew up a list of seven frequently used techniques, which are listed below along with brief explanations:

BANDWAGON *creating the impression of widespread support.*
CARD STACKING *playing up the facts supporting your side and vice versa.*
GLITTERING GENERALITIES *using vague but attractive words and sweeping statements.*
NAME CALLING *ridiculing the character and beliefs of the opposition.*
PLAIN FOLKS *using language and mannerisms to fit in with the audience.*
TESTIMONIAL *using a respected personality to make the point for you.*
TRANSFER *attaching something we respect, for example a flag, to the cause.*

These basic rules have been added to and complicated over time, but they remain a handy tool in unravelling the messages of our esteemed leaders today.

See also SPIN.

PUN

A pun is a humorous play on words, exploiting the ambiguity offered by words that sound alike or have more than one possible meaning. We've talked about prefixes: 'bad' is a common prefix for 'pun', since most of them are met with a groan.

There is no proof as to the origin of this cheeky little word, though the strongest theory is that it derives from the Italian *puntiglio*, meaning a fine point.

See also JOKES.

PYGMALION

'Words, words, words, I'm so tired of words'
'Show Me', *My Fair Lady*

Better known as *My Fair Lady*, the musical and the film into which it was adapted by Lerner and Loewe, *Pygmalion* is a play by George Bernard Shaw. It is about a phonologist, Professor Henry Higgins, who, for a bet, tries to change a Cockney flower girl, Eliza Doolittle, into a well-spoken lady by teaching her to alter the way in which she pronounces words. The title of the play comes from a story in 'Metamorphoses', a narrative poem by the Roman poet Ovid, in which Pygmalion is a sculptor who falls in love with a statue he has made.

Shaw's play opened in London in 1914 and he adapted it for the big screen in 1938. In 1956 it hit Broadway as a musical, featuring the famous song 'The Rain in Spain' ('Stays Mainly on the Plain'), and starring Julie Andrews as Eliza Doolittle and Rex Harrison as Professor Higgins. Eight years later the musical was made into a film, but Andrews' part went to Audrey Hepburn. Harrison won the Academy Award for Best Actor.

Qiviut, as any self-respecting textile merchant knows, is the underwool of the musk ox. What's remarkable about it is that it has managed to sneak into the *OED* without the usual credentials; that is, a 'u' after 'q'. The reason for 'q' and 'u'  sitting together as a digraph in most European languages is unknown.

Qiviut is one of a mere handful of common nouns in the *OED* that begin with a 'q' not followed by a 'u'. Here are the others, which will come in useful for Scrabble or Balderdash (see Games). Note the Albanian words. Albanian is one European language that evolved independently of the main Indo-European descendants.

> QAWWAL *a performer of qawwali* ♦ QAWWALI *a style of Muslim devotional music* ♦ QI *the life force according to Chinese philosophers* ♦ QIGONG *a system of exercises designed to strengthen the qi* ♦ QIN *a Chinese stringed instrument* ♦ QINDAR *a former monetary unit of Albania* ♦ QINDARKA *a current monetary unit of Albania* ♦ QINGHAOSU *a lactone used in the treatment of malaria* ♦ QIPAO *a Chinese dress*

Having said that, the various official Scrabble players' dictionaries offer some extra options.

> QABALAH *a mystical branch of Judaism* ♦ QADI *a judge* ♦ QAID, QAIDS *a chief or commander* ♦ QAIMAQAM *an official* ♦ QALAMDAN *a writing cabinet* ♦ QANAT, QANATS *a canal* ♦ QAT, QATS *a stimulant* ♦ QOPH, QOPHS 19th letter of the Hebrew alphabet* ♦ QWERTY, QWERTYS *a typewriter keyboard layout* ♦ QIBLA *cardinal direction for prayer*

Then, of course, there are words that include a 'q' without a 'u' within them, such as 'faqir' and 'sheqel', alternative spellings of 'fakir' and shekel' respectively.

READ

One of the great breakthroughs in human development was the ability to communicate ideas. The next step was to put those ideas down for others to read, but exactly when that first occurred has yet to be ascertained. Cave paintings, some of which date back more than 30,000 years, may have been our ancestors' attempts to tell each other something important – 'Next time you're down by the fast-moving wet thing, try to kill one of those big things with the pointy things on its top part; it tastes excellent if you hold it over the orange hot thing for a while and serve it with those roundish things that grow under the brown stuff that we move around on.' – or they might just have been decoration.

There's a gap of 24,000 years before the first known examples of 'writing' appear: the cuneiform figures pressed in clay by the Sumerians, which date to around 3200BC. Possibly older than these are the inscriptions on clay pots found in Harappa, Pakistan, which date back to around 3500BC.

The ancient Egyptians refined the inscriptions of the Sumerians and their hieroglyphs formed a highly sophisticated collection of literature. Ancient Egyptian was deciphered thanks to the Rosetta Stone, which was discovered in 1799. On the stone, written in 196BC, was an inscription which was a precursor of a modern-day instruction booklet, the sort of thing you get when you buy a new fridge, in that it was written in three scripts: hieroglyphic, demotic and Greek. The first was the formal language of Egypt, the second the common language and the third the ruling language. So the Rosetta Stone provided the key to deciphering hierogylphic and translating much ancient Egyptian writing.

The world's oldest 'book' – that is, a collection of pages held together – was discovered in a tomb in the Struma River valley, Bulgaria, in the middle of the last century. It consists of six pages of 24 carat gold, inscribed with text in Etruscan, a language that heavily influenced Latin before dying out. The book is 2,500 years old.

A manuscript dating from AD1000 bears the oldest known literary work in English, Beowulf. Written in Old English, Beowulf is an epic poem set in Scandinavia in the 5th century AD.

You would think by now that the ability to read would have become something we're born with, but it's not, far from it. In America, a 2003 survey, the National Assessment of Adult Literacy, revealed that 14 per cent of adults (30 million people) had 'Below Basic' prose literacy, and the number of proficiently literate white adults was falling.

RESTLESSNESS

Here's a word that is a noun derived from an adjective derived from a noun. It contains two Old English suffixes, 'less' and 'ness', attached to the Old English 'rest', the first of which forms an adjective and the second turns it back into a noun. It is also a good example of sibilance, which is the repeated emphasis of 's' or 'sh' sounds, and indeed rhyme.

See also ASSONANCE; RHYME

RETRONYM

Nouns like 'clock', 'television' and 'guitar' used to be very straightforward. They meant one thing and one thing alone. Then technology overtook them and the items we knew and loved had to be given an epithet to distinguish them from their more modern forms. A clock with hands and a face became an 'analogue clock' to distinguish it from a 'digital' one; television became 'terrestrial television' to distinguish it from the 'satellite' channels; and a guitar became an 'acoustic guitar' to distinguish it from an electric one.

Such names, invented after the item in question, are called retronyms – not to be confused with bacronyms (see Acronym).

RHYME

Although there is evidence of rhyming verse dating back 3,000 years in China, it didn't really catch on in Europe until the Irish made it popular in the Middle Ages. A 10th century book of Anglo-Saxon poetry features one poem written in rhyming couplets, but this is a rarity for the time. What John Milton called 'the invention of a barbarous age' began mostly as assonance, but developed during the second millennium AD into what we associate with rhyming today.

> *'Roses are red*
> *Violets are blue*
> *That doesn't rhyme*
> *But this sure do.'*

Sometimes you can see Milton's point; rhyming can restrict good poetry, but it can also add real power to it.

> *'Through the dense din, I say, we heard him shout*
> *"I see your lights!" But ours had long died out.'*
> 'The Sentry', Wilfred Owen

Or humour...

> *'Einstein can't be classed as witless*
> *He claimed atoms were the littlest*
> *When you did a bit of splitting-em-ness*
> *Frightened everybody sh**less.'*
> 'There Ain't Half Been Some Clever Bastards', Ian Dury & The Blockheads

Ian Dury's poetic device is an example of a 'feminine' rhyme, which is where the stress is placed on the penultimate syllable. A 'masculine' rhyme places the stress on the last syllable, like this:

> *'Humpty Dumpty sat on a wall*
> *Humpty Dumpty had a great fall'*

When the emphasis falls on the third to last syllable, it's called a dactylic rhyme. (If you're wondering whether this has anything to do with a pterodactyl, the dinosaur that terrorized the skies, it does. Pterodactyl means 'winged finger', *dactylus* being the Latin for finger, which has three joints.)

> *'A wonderful bird is a Pelican*
> *Whose beak can hold more than its belly can.'*

Not all rhymes are perfect. But that does not diminish the effect. Rapping, a genre that has taken rhyming to a new level, features assonance and consonance, 'oblique' rhymes where the sound is similar but not exact, and every other kind of rhyme imaginable. In 'Lose Yourself' by Eminem, he rhymes 'heavy', 'spaghetti', 'ready' and 'forgettin'. He rhymes words within the same line – 'nervous' and 'surface', 'reality', 'gravity' and 'Rabbit he' – giving the poetry a sense of relentlessly running on, almost tripping over itself. Beware, though; not all lyricists are as skilled as Eminem.

'I'm as serious as cancer *When I say rhythm is a dancer'*	'Rhythm is a Dancer', Snap
'Generals gathered in their masses *Just like witches at black masses'*	'War Pigs' (not a rhyme so much as repetition), Black Sabbath
'Can't complain, mustn't grumble *Help yourself to another piece* *of apple crumble'*	'That Was Then But This Is Now', ABC

See also ASSONANCE.

RHYTHM

Fine word though it is, 'rhythm' is one of those words that's commonly misspelt, mysteriously acquiring an 'n' at the end, like 'autumn'. The word 'rhythm' comes from the Latin *rhythmus*, also spelt *rithmus*, a term meaning 'measured motion' that was applied to accented verse. Because the two tended to go together, *rithmus* and *rime* (an Old French word) came to be synonymous, with 'rime' being the word to use. Then, in the 16th century, society's penchant for classical language and a misconception that 'rime' had originated not from Old French but from Latin, saw it changed by degrees to 'rhythm'. Later, the word 'rhyme' was coined to distinguish it from 'rhythm'.

Words have their own rhythm, formed by the combination of stressed and unstressed syllables, and moulded as an art form in poetry. The rhythm of poetry is called the meter and it breaks down into units called feet, of which there are five basic forms:

❶ ANAPEST *three syllables, accent on the third* ❷ DACTYL *three syllables, accent on the first* ❸ IAMB *two syllables, accent on the second* ❹ SPONDEE *two consecutive syllables, both stressed* ❺ TROCHEE *two syllables, accent on the first*

The meter is then defined as the number of syllabic feet in each line. One foot is a monometer, two feet a dimeter, three feet a trimeter, etc. The most well-known, the iambic pentameter, favoured by Shakespeare in his sonnets, has a meter of five iambic feet to the line, like this (accentuated syllables in bold):

*'Shall **I** com**pare** thee **to** a **sum**mer's **day**'*

See also RHYME; SPELLING; SYLLABLE.

RODOMONTADE

Next time you hear somebody getting too big for their boots, cut them down by accusing them of 'rodomontade'. It means extravagant bragging and boastfulness, and it came into English in the 16th century from Italian, where it had been derived through literature concerning the vainglorious (given to boastfulness) Saracen king Rodomont, a *braggadocio* (empty boaster and blusterer) if ever there was one. Funny how the ugly act of bragging has spawned such flamboyant words. The French spelling 'rodomontade' was adopted in the 17th century. Poet John Donne may have been the first to use the word in print in 1612: 'Challengers cartells, full of Rodomontades'.

ROGET, PETER (1779-1869)

Peter Mark Roget, of Swiss descent, was a physician who graduated from Edinburgh University and later founded Manchester University's School of Medicine and invented the log-log slide rule. His most famous work, however, created as something of a sideline, was *Roget's Thesaurus of English Words and Phrases*.

In 1805 Roget compiled a catalogue of words classified under generic headings as a personal aid to finding the most appropriate word for his own use. In short, it was a book of synonyms. Forty-seven years later, after some considerable expansion, his Thesaurus was published, the first book of its kind to offer similar and opposite words and expressions, sorted and classified together under six main headings.

❶ WORDS EXPRESSING ABSTRACT RELATIONS ❷ WORDS RELATING TO SPACE ❸ WORDS RELATING TO MATTER ❹ WORDS RELATING TO THE INTELLECTUAL FACULTIES ❺ WORDS RELATING TO THE VOLUNTARY POWERS ❻ WORDS RELATING TO THE SENTIENT AND MORAL POWERS

With these six classifications (since renamed and expanded to 15 categories), Roget created a template for sorting all the words and phrases in the English language into like groups. He took the most common words in each class to be the head word and included antonyms as well as synonyms, expanding this to words and phrases of similar meaning. For example, if you look up 'thesaurus' in the thesaurus you will find entries like 'dictionary', 'lexicon' and 'word book'. The word 'thesaurus' comes from the same Greek word that gives us 'treasure', Roget's thesaurus being a 'treasury' of words and phrases.

SAYINGS

An area that highlights the evolutionary nature of language and the issues that it throws up is the misquoting of well-known sayings. Here's another worm to coax the pedants out from under their rocks.

Listen to any sports programme for long enough and you are guaranteed to hear at least one player announce that he or she is 'chomping at the bit' in anticipation of the next contest. Whereupon, if there's a pedant in the room, they will say, 'Actually, that should be "champing at the bit", "to champ" meaning to chew vigorously or impatiently.' Thanks. Well, actually, so does chomp, and it has been used in the same context for 400 years.

Another example is 'parting shot'. Apparently, this phrase originated as 'Parthian shot', after the Parthians who ended their battles with the Romans by riding away at full speed while firing their arrows over their shoulders. But the Parthians, great though they were in their day, mean nothing to most people nowadays and 'parting shot' has exactly the same meaning.

However, misspoken words, phrases or sayings should be brought to book where the words do change the meaning, such as these common malapropisms.

Wrong	Should be
carry favour	curry favour (curry = groom) NB: not curry flavour!
far be it for me	far be it from me
free reign	free rein (rein = thing that controls a horse)
get your gander up	get your dander up (dander = an ember)
heart-rendering	heart-rending (rend = to tear)
pour over	pore over (pore = to look intently)
raise to the ground	raze to the ground (raze = obliterate)
short shift	short shrift (shrift = penance, in this case before execution)
show your metal	show your mettle (mettle = character)
step foot	set foot
tow the line	toe the line

You may not realize it, or care to admit to it, but it's likely that you know a thousand different sayings, some more common than others. If you take the trouble to list them all you'll find that this is a field that provides continuing employment for a host of words that would otherwise have been consigned to the scrapheap:

A pig in a poke ◆ *Devil take the hindmost* ◆ *Don't spoil the ship for a ha'p'orth of tar* ◆ *Done up like a popinjay* ◆ *Dressed to the nines* ◆ *He's not as green as he's cabbage looking* ◆ *Hide your light under a bushel* ◆ *In a quandary* ◆ *In one fell swoop* ◆ *Many a mickle makes a muckle* ◆ *Never the twain shall meet* ◆ *Nip and tuck* ◆ *On tenterhooks* ◆ *The whole kit and caboodle* ◆ *Warm the cockles of your heart*

See also CLICHÉ; MALAPROPISM.

SCRABBLE *see* GAMES

SEMANTICS

A word you often hear in relation to words and grammar, but what does it mean? Derived from the Greek *sema* (sign), from which we also get 'semaphore', semantics is the study of meaning, as affected by the structure of sentences. Not to be confused with syntax, which is the set of rules governing sentence structure. For example, 'I went to the boredom,' is syntactically correct because all the elements of the sentence – subject, verb, object – are arranged in the right order, but it is semantically incorrect because it makes no sense.

See also SYNTAX.

SHAKESPEARE, WILLIAM (1564-1616)

'Oh, that Shakespeare! What did he do? Nothing but string together a load of old clichés.' Groucho Marx

Not a bad wordsmith, Shakespeare: 37 plays, 154 sonnets, countless memorable lines, more quoted than *Monty Python*, Shakespeare was not just brilliant at putting words together, he also had a flair for making up his own. The expressions that he coined, or at least popularized, still punctuate our everyday language, as pertinent as if they were written yesterday.

○ *All's well that ends well*
○ *Breathe one's last*
○ *Eat out of house and home*
○ *Foregone conclusion*
○ *More sinned against than sinning*

○ *Neither rhyme nor reason*
○ *Pride of place*
○ *Tower of strength*
○ *Wear one's heart upon one's sleeve*
○ *Vanish into thin air*

Shakespeare was a master of the neologism – he is credited with about 2,000 – and knew every trick in the book. He coined his fair share of portmanteau words, like 'glister' and 'dwindle', as well as taking existing words and giving them a new twist. Here are some examples of his pioneering functional shifts (see Neologism):

'It will but skin and filme the ulcerous place.' 'FILM' AS A VERB
Hamlet, Act III Scene IV

'Next day after dawne.' 'DAWN' AS A NOUN *Henry V*, Act IV Scene I
'The bold windes speechlesse and the orbe below as hush as death.' 'HUSH' AS AN ADJECTIVE
Hamlet, Act II Scene II

Like the Greeks and the Romans, he liked to add prefixes and suffixes. By this method he created nouns like 'immediacy' and adjectives like 'eventful', 'lonely' and 'submerged' (from 'merge', which meant to dip or plunge). He based new words on Germanic influences ('hint', 'gust') as well as Latin ones ('frugal', 'castigate', 'articulate') and joined existing words together to form new compounds:

BAREFACED ❖ BEDROOM ❖ BLOODSTAINED ❖ EYEBALL ❖ FANCY-FREE ❖ LACKLUSTRE

Shakespeare coined neologisms that didn't stand the test of time. Words like 'incarnardine' (*Macbeth*), 'immoment' (*Antony and Cleopatra*), 'reprobance' (*Othello*) and 'irregulous' (*Cymbeline*). You could call it a scatter-gun approach, but his strike rate was remarkable.

See also CLICHÉ; COMPOUND; NEOLOGISM.

SHORTHAND

From as far back as the 4th century BC there is evidence that the Greeks were using vowel-based systems that enabled them to write faster. Shorthand, in some shape or form, has probably been around for almost as long as writing itself, the obvious question being why didn't they invent the language in shorthand in the first place?

The Roman consul Cicero had a secretary called Marcus Tullius Tiro, who invented a form of shorthand for writing his master's speeches. Known as Tironian notes, this system developed into a highly complex method that was widely used, particularly in monastic orders, until the 12th century AD. There are still remnants of Tironian notes in use today here and there. In English, the word 'viz', meaning 'namely' or 'that is to say', is an abbreviation of the Latin videlicet, the 'z' being a modified form of a Tironian symbol that represented that abbreviation.

In 16th century England the growing interest in writing sparked something of a shorthand rush, initiated by Timothy Bright's book *Characterie – An Arte of Shorte, Swifte and Secrete Writing by*

Straight Lines   p pl pr sp spr pt pn ps pns pb

Curves.   n nl nr sn nn ns nt ntr

Character. Ironically, he hadn't got round to dispensing with the 'e' on the end of 'shorte', 'swifte' and 'secrete' by that stage.

In 1837 Sir Isaac Pitman invented the most famous form of shorthand. The Pitman method is still in use today in its developed form. Pitman shorthand used symbols to represent sounds rather than letters, so 'f', 'gh' and 'ph', for example, would all have the same symbol. Vowels were optional, on the basis that most words could be deciphered from their consonants alone. Other shorthand methods have been devised which are easier to learn but not as quick to use. Stenographers trained in Pitman would be able to write upwards of 200 words per minute (the world record being a remarkable 350 wpm), whereas a simpler method, such as Teeline, might restrict them to around 150 wpm.

SILENT LETTERS

English is a language that's ripe for shorthand. Think of all those silent letters that you could get rid of straight away. The 'k' of knowledge, the 'g' of gnome, the 'b' of debt, the 'h' of honour, the 'p' of pneumonia... what on earth are they doing there in the first place?

There are various reasons why silent letters appear. The simplest explanation is that, in most cases, they haven't always been silent. The 'k' of knowledge and the 'gh' of 'night' used to be sounded in Old English. The 'p' of pneumonia indicates the Greek origin of the word; the 'h' of honour harks back to the Latin. In words like 'debt' and 'sign', links are maintained to the Latin origin (*debitum* and *signum*). Other silent letters actually help with pronunciation. For example, the 'u' in guess indicates that it should be pronounced with a hard 'g' and not as 'jess'. Confusing though the silent letters may be, once you can recognize where they've come from they actually give you a more thorough understanding of the language.

See also ASPIRATION.

SLANG

'Slang' is a word of unknown origin that only came into use in English about 250 years ago. Before then the special vocabulary used by specific social groups or professions was usually referred to as 'cant', from the Latin *cantus*, meaning song.

Slang generally serves two purposes: to build a sense of community amongst those who speak it and to alienate those who don't. To this end, most slang changes rapidly, with new words replacing old ones almost as fast as you can learn them. The obvious exception is Cockney rhyming slang. It has kept the same rhymes for 'feet' (plates of meat) and 'stairs' (apples and pears) for at least 150 years.

In *The Slang Dictionary or The Vulgar Words, Street Phrases and 'Fast' Expressions of High and Low Society*, compiled by John Camden Hotten in 1860, he writes, 'I learn that the rhyming slang was introduced about twelve or fifteen years ago.' But its roots in the slang of thieves date back to the 16th century.

The beauty of rhyming slang is that the principle is so simple, anyone can make up new words. New expressions are added all the time. When the late Ayrton Senna rose to fame in motor racing, he at last gave the language a rhyme for a ten pound note (Ayrton Senna: tenner). Similarly, in the 1960s the Irish singer Ruby Murray provided a handy rhyme for Britain's favourite food, the curry. Her modern counterpart, Britney Spears, is now rhyming slang for beers. 'If you've got a spare Ayrton we can go for a few Britneys followed by a Ruby.'

Youth slang moves so fast it would be foolish to try to list examples of it here; they'd be laughably out of date by the time you read this. Instead, here are some examples of street slang from the mid-1800s, as listed in *The Slang Dictionary*. Some of these words are still in regular use but with very different meanings; others have survived intact.

Slang word ⟹	Meaning		
ALL THERE ⟹	*first rate*	FROG ⟹	*policeman*
BAGS ⟹	*trousers*	FRUMP ⟹	*mock or insult*
BANDED ⟹	*hungry*	GAMMY ⟹	*bad*
BLOWER ⟹	*girlfriend*	GOB ⟹	*portion*
BONE ⟹	*to steal*	GROGGY ⟹	*inebriated*
CAB ⟹	*to stick together*	GRUBBY ⟹	*old-fashioned*
CASCADE ⟹	*to vomit*	HIPPED ⟹	*annoyed*
CHEESY ⟹	*fine or showy*	HUMP ⟹	*to spoil*
CHUCK UP ⟹	*to surrender*	KOOTEE ⟹	*house*
COD ⟹	*to wind up*	RIG ⟹	*frolic or spree*
DAMAGE ⟹	*amount payable*	RUM ⟹	*weird*
DOWNER ⟹	*sixpence*	VAGABOND ⟹	*tramp or beggar*
FOXY ⟹	*red-haired*		

SO

This simple, two-letter adverb has become one of the verbal phenomena of the early 21st century, thanks in no small part to American sitcom *Friends*. It actually has numerous definitions, but the one that has become used almost to breaking point is 'to a great or notable degree', as in 'I am so cold', but coupled with a negative, for example 'I am so not cold,' or with a verb, for example 'I so do.'

In this case 'I am not cold at all' would have conveyed the same message, although perhaps not as emphatically, and 'I am so warm' doesn't convey the same message. So there is a practical argument for using 'so not', particularly when coupled with some slang phrase for which there is no readily available opposite, for example 'I am so not into that.' How could you rephrase that? 'I am so out of that'? Hardly.

See also ANTONYM.

SOLECISM

Defined by *The OED* as 'a violation of the rules of grammar or syntax', solecism is a word seldom used other than by writers of books about the misuse of the English language – who use it incessantly. Commonplace examples include the use of 'I' instead of 'me' and vice versa, and the use of 'of' instead of 'have' in the past conditional tense.

See also I; OF.

SONGS

The quest to find the right words to express the deep-seated passions that drive the songwriter can be a long and winding road, and inevitably this quest has become the actual subject of the song on several occasions.

'Poetic licence' is common amongst songwriters and indeed they are among the biggest influences on the development of language through slang.

It should be noted that not all songs have words. Felix Mendelssohn wrote a series of eight compositions, each consisting of six 'songs' for piano only, and he called these *Lieder ohne Worte* (Songs Without Words).

HERE ARE TEN SONGS THAT DO INCLUDE WORDS:

❶ *'It's Only Words'* THE BEE GEES ❷ *'Missing Words'* THE SELECTER ❸ *'Sorry Seems to be the Hardest Word'* ELTON JOHN ❹ *'The Word'* THE BEATLES ❺ *'Word Up'* CAMEO ❻ *'Words'* THE MONKEES ❼ *'Words Don't Come Easy To Me'* F.R. DAVID ❽ *'Words Get In The Way'* MIAMI SOUND MACHINE ❾ *'Words of Love'* MAMAS & THE PAPAS ❿ *'Words You Say'* MOODY BLUES

See also LIBRETTO.

SPEECH

Until recently it was believed that humans developed the power of speech about 160,000 years ago, but a recent archaeological find in Spain threw up evidence to suggest that predecessors of the Neanderthals who lived about 350,000 years ago had the faculty of speech. The clue lies in the construction of the inner ear, which enables the listener to hear sounds in the 2–4 kHz frequency range, which contains the relevant acoustic information for speech.

Oratory, the art of making speeches, was regarded as an important skill by the Greeks and the Romans. In these days of the soundbite, great speeches are a rarity, but when leaders had the time to develop their message and audiences were prepared to listen, some legendary words were spoken that will live forever in history.

'I know I have but the body of a weak and feeble woman; but I have the heart of a king, and of a king of England too...'
Queen Elizabeth I, preparing to fight the Spanish Armada

✳

'Let us, therefore, brace ourselves to our duties and so bear ourselves that if the British Empire and its Commonwealth last for a thousand years, men will still say, "This was their finest hour." '
Winston Churchill, as Germany occupies France

✳

'I have a dream that one day on the red hills of Georgia the sons of former slaves and the sons of former slave owners will be able to sit down together at the table of brotherhood. I have a dream.'
Martin Luther King Jr, Washington demonstration

Correct spelling is crucial to the understanding of worms. You see, by misspelling 'words' as 'worms' we give the sentence a different meaning altogether. There are those, however, who fly in the face of the self-appointed guardians of proper English and claim that correct spelling is seldom vital to understanding the intended meaning of a sentence. Here's one example: 'The children were very pleased with there presents.' This should say 'their' presents rather than 'there' presents, but nobody could be confused by this.

In American English, words such as centre and honour have been given new, more simple spellings – center and honor – along modern phonetic lines. Nevertheless, correct spelling is still regarded as important to preserve order in the language and to avoid confusing words with worms.

Accomodating Brocolli in the Cemetary by Vivian Cook has a page devoted to what it calls 'difficult' words. Why do so many people find certain words so difficult to spell? Cook cites the following:

DOUBLE CONSONANTS
* BROCCOLI not *brocolli*
* CARIBBEAN not *Carribean*
* MEDITERRANEAN not *Meditteranean*
* MISSISSIPPI not *Misissipi*
* PICCADILLY not *Picaddily*

CONFUSED VOWELS
* CEMETERY not *cemetary*
* DEFINITE not *definate*
* MINUSCULE not *miniscule*
* SEPARATE not *seperate*

WORDS WITH THE SAME SPELLING OR SOUND
* STATIONARY (not moving) and *stationery* (pens, paper, etc.)
* THERE, THEIR and THEY'RE

MAKING UNUSUAL SPELLINGS REGULAR
* ECSTASY not *ecstacy*
* INOCULATE not *innoculate*
* SACRILEGIOUS not *sacreligious*
* SUPERSEDE not *supercede*

> ## SPIN
>
> Spin is the act of giving a twisted interpretation of, say, a statement or an event in order to sway public opinion; spin has become the keystone of politics and commerce, having entered common usage in the 1980s. The public is now so aware (and tired) of spin, that spin doctors (those who do the spinning) have invented new terms to describe their dubious art, such as 'transformation strategy'.

See also EUPHEMISM; PROPAGANDA; VERBOSITY.

SPOONERISM

'I'd rather have a bottle in front o' me than a frontal lobotomy.'

The above quote is a deliberate Spoonerism, often attributed to Dorothy Parker. Spoonerism itself is an eponym. It was the Reverend William Archibald Spooner, the legendary Dean of New College, Oxford, who gave his name to the word. He was renowned for a speech impediment that caused him to swap letters or syllables in a word or phrase, thus rendering a completely different meaning upon what he was trying to say. *The Oxford Dictionary of Quotations* gives this example:

> *'The weight of rages will press hard upon the employer.'*
> (Instead of 'The rate of wages...')

Other, unconfirmed examples, are funnier. 'You have hissed all of my mystery lessons' (missed all of my history lessons) and 'You have tasted two worms' (wasted two terms).

Spoonerisms abound in popular culture, where they are used for comic effect.

See also EPONYM.

SPORTING WORDS

The world of sport has an aptitude for jargon and cliché that takes some beating, as well as its own particular use of tenses – 'I've hit the freekick and Mickey's run in and he's headed it past the keeper.' But in addition to the singular use of common English and the reinventing of familiar words – for example 'result' has come to mean a win, and 'ask' is now a noun, as in 'big ask' – sport has a technical vocabulary all of its own.

TRACK AND FIELD

BATON *from the Old French* baston – *a stick used as a weapon or a symbol of office.*

DISCUS *Latin word derived from the Greek* diskos – *a quoit.*

HURDLE *from the Old English* hyrdel – *a temporary fence of woven sticks.*

JAVELIN *from the French* javeline – *a light spear.*

STEEPLECHASE *as with horse racing, derived from a tradition of racing to a church steeple on horseback and having to jump all obstacles in the way.*

TENNIS

ACE *from Old French* as – *the one on a dice.*

DEUCE *from Old French* deus – *two.*

LET *from Old English* lettan – *to hinder.*

LOVE *from the French* l'oeuf – *the egg, due to its shape.*

UMPIRE *transformation of 'noumpere' ('a noumpere' becoming 'an oumpere'), from the Old French* nonper – *without equal.*

EQUESTRIANISM

CHUKKA *from Hindi* Chakar – *a circle or turn.*

DRESSAGE *French word for training.*

PUISSANCE *French word for power.*

GOLF

BIRDIE *from 19th century American slang: 'bird', meaning cool.*

EAGLE *a bigger birdie (2 under par).*

ALBATROSS *an even bigger birdie (3 under par).*

BOGEY *originally used in Britain to mean the perfect score, but later came to mean one over par – the score an amateur might shoot for – as 'par' became the term for the perfect pro score.*

CADDIE *from 'cadee', a form of the French* cadet.

DIVOT *from Scottish dialect, meaning a turf.*

DORMIE *said to be from Scottish slang for dormouse, a sign of good luck, or else possibly from the French* dormir *– to sleep.*

HANDICAP *shortened version of 'hand in the cap'.*

LINKS *from 'linksland', a Scottish term for the sandy grassland near the seashore.*

PAR *Latin word meaning that which is equal to.*

STYMIE *from Scottish 'styme' – something that can barely be seen.*

YIPS *20th century neologism attributed to golfer Tommy Armour.*

ICE HOCKEY

PUCK *believed to come from Irish word* poc *– to hit.*

RINK *from Old French* renc *– a row or rank; the ground where jousting took place.*

GENERAL

AGGREGATE *from Latin* aggregatus *– united in a flock.*

BOUT *from Old English* byht *– to bow or bend, giving the sense of a round.*

HEAT *from sense of 'to make hot' with one blast of fire, giving a single bout of effort.*

RUBBER *old bowls term of unknown origin, but possibly connected to 'rub' – an obstacle or hindrance.*

STEREO

Most of us know the word 'stereo' from the hi-fi in the living room. Because it splits the sound through two channels, as opposed to mono (from the Greek *monos*, meaning one), we might assume that the 'stereo' part of 'stereophonic' means 'two'. But, in fact, the Greek root word *stereos* means solid or three-dimensional.

The clue to this is in the word 'stereotype', which is a printing term for when type is cast in a solid mould for repeated use. Hence a stereotypical person is someone who conforms to a fixed character type. Given that relatively few people have ever worked in the print business, its terminology has seeped into the wider language remarkably well. In addition to stereotype, common words and phrases that have come directly from the print shop include:

DOG EAR *fold in the paper.* ❖ FONT *a complete set of a particular style of type; from the French fondre (to found or cast).* ❖ HEADLINE *title line at the top of a story.* ❖ LOWER CASE *small letters, stored in the lower section.* ❖ TYPE-CAST *formed into type for printing.* ❖ UPPER CASE *capital letters, stored in the upper section of the type cabinet.*

SUFFIX

Just as a prefix is an element added to the beginning of a word to modify its meaning, a suffix is an element added to the end for the same purpose. The first part of the word is actually an altered form of the Latin prefix sub, meaning below or under, indicating that the suffix plays a secondary role to the main part of the word. Such variations of the prefix sub exist in many words where you might not suspect it. When attached to words beginning with 'm', 'r', 'c', 'f', 'g' or 'p', the 'b' of 'sub' tended to change to the first letter of that word. Hence summon, surrogate, succeed, suffer, suggest and supply are all formed from the prefix 'sub'.

Suffixes are evident in most words in English, although some are more obvious than others. The least obvious are those that indicate tense or person, such as the past 'ed' and the plural 's'. Then there are those that change the function of a word, for example:

NOUN TO VERB

● FY ⅀⧽ *liquid* to *liquify* ● ISE/IZE ⅀⧽ *maximum* to *maximise*

VERB TO NOUN

● MENT ⅀⧽ *entertain* to *entertainment*

VERB TO ADJECTIVE

● ABLE/IBLE ⅀⧽ *drink* to *drinkable*
● IST ⅀⧽ *baptise* to *baptist*

ADJECTIVE TO NOUN

● ISM ⅀⧽ *modern* to *modernism*

● NESS ⅀⧽ *sweet* to *sweetness*

ADJECTIVE TO ADVERB

● LY ⅀⧽ *quick* to *quickly*

NOUN TO ADJECTIVE

● FUL ⅀⧽ *joy* to *joyful*
● IC ⅀⧽ *scene* to *scenic*
● ISH ⅀⧽ *Swede* to *Swedish*
● OUS ⅀⧽ *nebula* to *nebulous*

Many of these suffixes come from Greek or Latin. Here are some of the more obvious suffixes we've inherited from the ancients, and what they mean to us:

	FROM	MEANING
●*arium/ orium*	LATIN	*place of*
●*cide*	LATIN	*killer*
●*cracy*	GREEK	*to rule*
●*graphy*	GREEK	*to write*
●*logy*	GREEK	*words*
●*mania*	LATIN	*excessive desire*
●*phobe*	GREEK	*fearing*
●*phone*	GREEK	*sound*
●*scope*	LATIN	*to look at*

See also GREEK; LATIN; PREFIX.

SURNAMES

Surnames are a consequence of a growth in population. Before William conquered Britain in 1066, there weren't any surnames to pass down from one generation to the next. People were known by a single name, one that described them specifically, such as Bear-crusher, or Big-nose. But as communities grew the same village might then have two Big-noses amongst its inhabitants so it became necessary to add detail, for example Big-nose the Butcher and Big-nose the Baker.

Surnames arose that identified people in different ways: their father's name (Johnson); their occupation (butcher); some feature of where they lived (Woods); or some other physical attribute (Small). Our surnames offer a clue to the character of our ancestors. Take the ten most common names in Britain.

NAME	MEANING	NAME	MEANING
BROWN	hair or skin colour (Old English)	TAYLOR	cutter of cloth (Middle English)
DAVIES	son of David (biblical)	THOMAS	son of Thomas (biblical)
EVANS	son of Evan or Ifan, the Welsh version of John (biblical)	WILLIAMS	son of William (after William the Conqueror)
JONES	son of John (biblical)	WILSON	son of William (popularized by William the Conqueror)
ROBERTS	son of Robert (Germanic)		
SMITH	metal worker (Old English)		

All but three mean 'son of'. But William the Conqueror, whose dominion after 1066 popularized the name in Britain, got his name (Guillaume in French) from the Germanic Wilhelm, which does have a meaning: *wil* means desire and *helm* means helmet or protection. Similarly John comes from a Hebrew word meaning 'gift of God' and Thomas is derived from an Aramaic word meaning 'twin'. The inventiveness is there after all. After ancestral names, the most common source of surnames is occupations. In addition to Smith and Taylor we find:

✳ BAILEY *an official of the crown* ✳ CARTER *a carrier of goods* ✳ CLARKE *a clerk or cleric* ✳ COOK *from Old English 'coc', a cook* ✳ COOPER *a barrel-maker* ✳ PARKER *a gamekeeper* ✳ TURNER *a lathe worker* ✳ WALKER *from Middle English 'walkcere', a person who walked on raw cloth to thicken it, an occupation from which we also get the name Fuller* ✳ WARD *from Old English 'weard', a guard or watchman* ✳ WRIGHT *from Old English 'wryhta', a craftsman*

SYLLABLE

You don't need to be told what syllables are, but it is worth taking a moment to recognize what they do for words and language. These single-beat blocks of sound are what give words their character. They organize themselves within words into an order of importance which is marked out by the emphasis placed on them.

This in turn affects rhythm and rhyme. The meter of poetry is determined by the number of syllables in each line and it is the stressed syllables that are considered as the basis of rhyme. For example, excitement and enjoyment are not considered to rhyme even though they both end in 'ment'.

There are three parts to the structure of a syllable: the onset, the nucleus and the coda. Not all syllables have an onset or a coda, but they all have a nucleus, usually the vowel sound, for example the 'ea' of seat. In this instance the 's' is the onset of the syllable (the consonant sound that precedes the nucleus) and the 't' is the coda (the consonant sound that follows it). In 'sea' there is no coda, and in 'eat' there is no onset.

See also RHYME; RHYTHM.

SYNONYM

The antonym of antonym is synonym, from the Greek *syn*, meaning 'with', and *onoma*, meaning 'name' – a word that means the same thing as another word. English has an abundance of synonyms, a consequence of being derived from several parent languages. In most cases you have the choice of a short Anglo-Saxon word and a long Latinate one. Here are some extreme examples:

fun RECREATION ✱ *house* RESIDENCE ✱ *job* EMPLOYMENT ✱ *meet* ENCOUNTER ✱ *nice* ENJOYABLE ✱ *say* ARTICULATE ✱ *try* ENDEAVOUR ✱ *weird* UNUSUAL

See also ANTONYM; ROGET.

SYNTAX

Syntax is the study of how words work together through their arrangement in a sentence, as well as the rules governing that arrangement. Syntax governs the way different parts of speech are ordered. 'Go I the shops to,' is syntactically incorrect. English syntax dictates that the subject 'I' should come before the verb 'go' and the preposition 'to' should come before the object 'the shops'. Syntax works closely with semantics to make sense of the words we speak and write.

See also SEMANTICS.

TAUTOLOGY

From the Greek *tauto* (the same) and *logos* (saying), tautology is the unnecessary use of words or phrases that mean or imply the same thing. It begins in childhood – the 'big, huge monster' – and thrives in marketing and political language, probably a consequence of trying too hard to push an idea. 'Product offerings', for example, is a phrase you see a lot these days. But there's no need for the word 'offerings'; 'product' is enough on its own. And here's George Bush giving us a shining example of tautology in his political rhetoric.

> *'My job is a decision-making job and, as a result, I make a lot of decisions.'*

It's an extremely erudite person who always avoids tautology, especially when some tautological terms have become such familiar parts of speech as these examples:

ADVANCE BOOKING ❖ BRIEF SUMMARY ❖ FELLOW TEAM-MATES ❖ REVERT BACK ❖ SAFE HAVEN ❖ SUBTLE NUANCES

Sometimes tautology is used deliberately to emphasize a point, for example 'free gift', whereby the word 'free' is implied by the word 'gift', yet it removes any doubt over the conditions attached to the gift. Unless it's a free gift offered by a timeshare company, of course.

TEENAGER

Arguably the most powerful neologism of the 20th century, 'teenager' derived from a term that had been in use for centuries, 'the teens', and became the label for a cultural phenomenon. The practice of lumping all youths aged 13–19 together under one label dates back to at least the 17th century. But the noun 'teen-ager' did not appear in print until 1941 and remained rarely used until the 1950s. At this point, postwar American youth made the most of a degree of freedom and prosperity unknown to previous generations by establishing their own style of dress, music, language and behaviour.

By the end of the 1950s, everybody knew what a teenager was. The term has survived the passage of time unscathed and is still the best word for those 'difficult years' between childhood and adulthood.

TERMS OF ENDEARMENT

The words we use for the ones we love should perhaps be kept behind closed doors. It's a private matter. But where do these words come from? Food plays a large part in the more common terms of endearment, as do flora and fauna, but you have to choose carefully.

☺ Good	☹ Bad	☺ Good	☹ Bad
☺ blossom	☹ sap	☺ kitten	☹ horse
☺ bunny	☹ weasel	☺ lambkin	☹ cow
☺ buttercup	☹ pansy	☺ peachy	☹ cheesy
☺ cupcake	☹ fruitcake	☺ petal	☹ thorn
☺ cutiepie	☹ pork pie	☺ pumpkin	☹ cabbage
☺ duck	☹ cock	☺ pussycat	☹ dog
☺ honey	☹ porridge	☺ sugar	☹ salt
☺ honeypie	☹ stew	☺ sweet pea	☹ wort

TEXTING LANGUAGE

The mobile phone has made many changes to the way we live, not least of which is the introduction of a whole new language. Thanks to mobile phone texting or SMS (Short Message Service), words like 'lol', 'omg' and 'roflmao' have entered the English language. In the pursuit of speed, and in order to fit more information into the character limit imposed by most SMS systems, texting has spawned its own shorthand. This is made up of abbreviations, vowel displacement and phonetic replacements that are quite easy to learn and even easier to use. Here are some famous phrases translated into text language.

AL 4 1 & 1 4 AL   2 B O NOT 2 B   C U L8R ALLIGATOR

It's not too difficult to figure out what these mean, once you understand that individual numbers and letters like '2', '4', '8', 'b', 'c', 'u', 'r' and 'y' replace their phonetic syllabic equivalent, but text language has grown far beyond these simple examples. LOL, for example, has for years been an abbreviation for 'lots of love', but now it stands for 'laughing out loud'. Even more esoteric, ROFL stands for 'rolling on the floor laughing' and ROFLMAO means 'rolling on the floor laughing my ass off'.

All users are naturally going to introduce their own words into the texting vocabulary and yet, rather than branching out into a million different languages, useful new words quickly become standard and one language is evolving.

Other longstanding acronyms such as TTFN (tata for now) and SWALK (sealed with a loving kiss) live on, and you might guess correctly at some of the more fashionable phrases that have been textified, such as OMG (oh my god, or omigod) and KWIM (know what I mean), but what about SHID (slaps head in disgust) or YYSSW (yeah yeah sure sure whatever).

> *'The razor-toothed piranhas of the genera Serrasalmus and Pygocentrus are the most ferocious freshwater fish in the world. In reality they seldom attack a human.'*

This is the standard phrase set by the *Guinness Book of World Records* for contestants wishing to text their way into the record books. It must be typed without predictive text or spelling aids. In December 2006, Ben Cook of Utah, United States, set a record time of 41 seconds.

Once you have got up to speed and are fluent in the language of texting, the world is your oyster. But beware: like email, texting is a dangerous flirtation tool and it is often tempting to show off your SMS fluency when you've had a few to drink. 'Intexticating', as it is called, is now recognized as the biggest cause of embarrassment in the workplace.

THE

The most commonly used word in English, 'the', also known as the definite article, is one of the trickier words to grasp for people learning English, and not just because of the pronunciation of 'th'. Many languages don't have articles, so learning when to say 'the' or 'a' or 'some' is an entirely alien concept. The way we use 'the' is complex and very hard to define. For example, 'I'm in hospital' means something different to 'I'm in the hospital'. Leave out the definite article and it indicates that you're talking about more than just the place; you're implying the whole treatment process associated with hospitals. It makes you wonder how great languages like Latin, Sanskrit, Persian and Homeric Greek got by without the definite article. As a general rule, 'the' is used about something both unique and familiar. We attach it without really thinking to the names of things, such as ships, planes and trains – the *Titanic*, the *Flying Scotsman* – even though their names do not actually include 'the'. It bestows that sense of uniqueness that a title requires.

NEWSPAPERS	BANDS	COUNTRIES
The Daily Telegraph	The Beatles	*The Congo*
Le Monde (The World)	The Clash	*The Gambia*
El Pais (The Nation)	The Crickets	*The Ivory Coast*
The Sun	The Rolling Stones	*The Netherlands*
The Times	The Sex Pistols	*The Philippines*
The Wall Street Journal	... and inevitably	*The Sudan*
The Washington Post	The The	*The United States*

In 2006 the Oxford University Press surveyed the Internet to find the most commonly used English words. Of the top 100, 90 per cent were monosyllabic and mostly derived from Old English. In spite of all the changes, it's still the old Anglo-Saxon words that get used the most.

THESAURUS *see* ROGET

THEY

Versatile though the English language is, there is one gaping hole that is becoming increasingly bothersome. When referring to somebody of either sex in the third person singular, there is no word that satisfactorily does the job. 'It' is too impersonal. 'They', the third person plural, has to fill in. In years gone by, before we realized that it might be offensive to women, it was acceptable to use the masculine as a matter of course:

'He who laughs last laughs longest.'

But sexual equality in the late 20th century meant that the cumbersome 'he or she' came into use. It hardly solved the problem:

'Let he or she who is without sin cast the first stone.'

Now academics in the United States are claiming that the word 'yo' is gradually becoming an accepted replacement for 'he or she'. In 2007 a paper was published in the quarterly publication *American Speech*, entitled 'A New Gender-Neutral Pronoun in Baltimore, Maryland: A Preliminary Study'. Between 2004 and 2007 its authors, Elaine M. Stotko and Margaret Troyer, gathered examples of 'yo' used in place of both 'he' and 'she' in the language of school pupils. What the examples published don't seem to include is instances of 'yo' in place of 'he or she', but as it was used in place of both terms separately it is clearly gender-neutral. This raised the hope that 'yo' might become the missing link that the English language has been crying out for. Given the spread rate of American slang around the world, this is entirely possible.

See also ONE.

TIME

According to the OUP survey mentioned under the 'The' heading, the noun that gets the most use in English is 'time'. This is not surprising, considering the amount of time we spend worrying about how little time we have. Interestingly, three more nouns in the top ten are words pertaining to time, if you include 'life' in that category:

1 time **2** person **3** year **4** way **5** day **6** thing
7 man **8** world **9** life **10** hand

See also THE.

TONGUE-TWISTER

'Through three cheese trees three free fleas flew.
While these fleas flew, freezy breeze blew.
Freezy breeze made these three trees freeze.
Freezy trees made these trees' cheese freeze.
That's what made these three free fleas sneeze.'
Dr Seuss, 'Fox in Socks'

Why do some combinations of words trip off the tongue while others tie your tongue up in knots? Great writers and orators choose their words carefully for ease of diction as well as sense, for a phrase that is pleasing to say is also pleasing to hear.

Others, like Dr Seuss, go to the opposite extreme. In this instance he played on the difficulty we have when a lot of 'f's are pronounced close together. The famous scoreline from Scottish football, 'East Fife 4, Forfar 5' is a classic example of this. Another tricky combination is 'l' and 'r': 'red lorry, yellow lorry'.

Harder still is the combination of 's' sounds and 'sh' sounds in close proximity.
'She sells seashells by the sea shore.' Try saying these without your teeth in.

✱ *The sixth sick sheikh's sixth sheep's sick.*

✱ *Is this your sister's sixth zither, sir?*

✱ *Three free throws.*

✱ *Lesser leather never weathered wetter weather better.*

✱ *Flee from fog to fight flu fast!*

✱ *We surely shall see the sun shine soon.*

✱ *Moose noshing much mush.*

✱ *One smart fellow, he felt smart. Two smart fellows, they felt smart. Three smart fellows, they all felt smart.*

TYPEWRITER

The development of the typewriter in the 19th century forced a closer inspection of the ways in which words were formed. In the race to invent the first marketable typewriter, many weird and wonderful contraptions were tried and tested, but it was American inventor Christopher Sholes who cracked it, along with Carlos Glidden and Samuel W. Soule. Fundamental to the success of their invention was the seemingly random 'qwerty' keyboard layout, which remains the standard to this day. Sholes conceived this keyboard layout to overcome the problem of keys jamming together during rapid typing. He got teacher Amos Densmore, the brother of his chief backer, to study how words were formed and then make a note of the letters that frequently appeared consecutively. Then he rearranged the original alphabetical keyboard so that the keys for these letters were positioned sufficiently far apart in the carriage so as not to catch. Remington

 produced this first keyboard in 1874, but it wasn't until the second edition model came out four years later that sales really took off. The difference? The facility to type both upper and lower case letters, by way of a key that 'shifted' the carriage up so that a different part of the type key hit the paper.

UN VS. IN

Ever wondered why we have

UNBELIEVABLE	*but*	INEXPLICABLE
UNFRIENDLY	*but*	INHOSPITABLE
UNINITIATED	*but*	INEXPERIENCED
UNKIND	*but*	INSINCERE
UNWANTED	*but*	INVOLUNTARY

The simple differentiation is that 'un-' is of Germanic descent while 'in-' is from Latin. Both originated in the Indo-European 'n-', which was used to give a negative inflexion to the word it attached to. But who decided which to use where?

Up until the 14th century the Germanic 'un-' was always used. Then, as scholars began to plump up the language with the liberal use of Latin words, the prefix 'in-' came into use, particularly when applied to words of Latin origin. Even so, 'in-' was used as an alternative, rather than a replacement, for the Germanic forms: so you could say 'incapable' or 'uncapable', 'inarticulate' or 'unarticulate'.

The use of the negative prefix expanded rapidly over the next 300 years as the English vocabulary grew. It was affixed to just about any adjective or adverb, with the exception of shorter Germanic ones such as 'good' and 'bad', which generally had a simple antonym already.

Come the 17th century and there were so many of these 'either or' words floating around that linguists decided it was time to make some hard decisions. Many words with Latin roots were given the 'in-' prefix exclusively, while the rest went off with 'un-'. 'Un-' remained the most common of the two and its use has continued to expand right up to the present day.

The Latin 'in-' is also less common because it changes form before certain consonants, to aid pronunciation.

IL- BEFORE L	⟹	*illegal, illogical*
IM- BEFORE P AND M	⟹	*imperfect, immature*
IR- BEFORE R	⟹	*irreligious, irrespective*

VERB

We get the word 'verb' via Old French from the Latin *verbum*, meaning word or verb. The *OED* definition of a verb requires you to look up several other words in order to understand it, so let's just call it a 'doing' word. In grammar, a verb is one of the essentials that make up a sentence, along with the subject noun. For just about every object or condition it is possible to create a verb, either by adding the suffix '-ize' or by the process of functional shift, whereby the word remains the same but assumes a new syntactic job. Adjectives like 'clear' and 'clean', for example, also work as verbs. Imaginative wordsmiths like William Shakespeare (see Shakespeare) realized that you could create very evocative verbs in this way.

> *'This day shall gentle his condition'*
> Henry V, Act IV Scene III

Today, everybody's at it, especially in the business world:

* 'We'll *leverage* our combined abilities going forward.' (make maximum use of)
* 'The boss has *tasked* me with improving efficiency.' (assign a task)
* 'OK, we'll *action* that first thing in the morning.' (put into practice)
* 'Have they *dogfooded* the product yet?' (taste one's own product)
* 'We can't go on *bank-rolling* them forever.' (support financially)
* 'James is *ballparking* the sums involved right now.' (come up with a rough amount)
* 'Let's *birdtable* the agenda over coffee.' (meet and discuss)
* 'Can you *gist* the report for us please, Sarah?' (précis)
* '*Pulse* your contacts for their views on the takeover.' (gather opinion or information)
* 'I think it's time to *sunset* the entire range.' (gradually wind down)
* 'We're *transitioning* to a new IT system.' (change)
* 'There's a *visioning* session planned for Monday morning.' (brainstorm)

VERBOSITY

The love of words is a fine thing, but using them sparingly is the best way to express that love. Verbosity (using more words than necessary) is a misleading device. It is often used to give the impression of intellectual superiority, particularly when related to the use of long words that the listener is unlikely to know. It is also used to give the impression that something of great significance is being said when in fact it isn't. Verbosity has become a major weapon in politics and marketing, the two institutions that compete most fiercely for media space. It was said of Clement Atlee, British PM (1945–51), that he would never use one word where none would do. But for today's politicians, verbosity is an important skill. It is fundamental to the art of not answering the question.

'It would be dishonest to say I'd rule out indefinitely the office you refer to.'
Gordon Brown

It also creates the impression that the decisions you've taken are more complex – and therefore less likely to be questioned by the general public – than they really are.

'We'll be sending a person on the ground there pretty soon to help implement the malaria initiative.'
George W. Bush

And ultimately it can be used to create utter confusion, thus distracting attention from whatever the real issue was in the first place.

'There are known knowns. These are things we know that we know. There are known unknowns. That is to say, there are things we know we don't know. But, there are also unknown unknowns. These are things we don't know we don't know.'
Donald Rumsfeld

See also PROPAGANDA; TAUTOLOGY.

VOCABULARY

In short, a vocabulary is defined as a list of words. However, the term is more often seen as referring to the complete range of words understood by a person or group of people, or the words existing in any given language. Having been fed by so many other languages, English is believed to have a larger vocabulary than any other language, with an estimated three-quarters of a million words.

But how many of these are we expected to know? Well, maybe not *lomentaceous*, *pantoyl* or *trotty*, but Professor David Crystal, author of *The Cambridge Encyclopedia of the English Language*, believes you're unlikely to find anybody with an active vocabulary of fewer than 35,000 words. That is, the range of words you use when speaking or writing. In addition to that we have an even larger passive vocabulary – the range of words we understand but do not use – bringing our overall vocabulary to at least 75,000 words. In fact, Crystal estimates that the average college graduate has a vocabulary of 135,000 words, of which 60,000 are in their active vocabulary and 75,000 passive.

Studies into infant speech have found we develop a passive vocabulary before an active one; in other words we start to recognize words before we utter any coherent ones of our own. That usually happens at around the age of 12 months. By 18 months a child will have on average around 20 words in their active vocabulary, rising to around 50 by the age of two years. But they will be able to understand far more than they can say.

By the age of five years a child's vocabulary will have soared to over 2,000 words.

Studies have found that around 85 per cent of what we say is made up of just a few hundred words. This 'core' vocabulary consists mainly of pronouns, articles, adverbs, adjectives, prepositions and verbs – the nuts and bolts of language. There are very few nouns in this core vocabulary.

VOWEL

A vowel is the sound produced by air passing over the vocal chords, thereby causing them to vibrate. Unlike consonants, which need a vowel sound with them to form a syllable, vowels require no other vocal movement to make a sound.

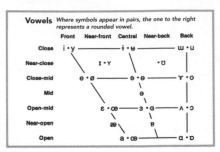

The International Phonetic Alphabet (IPA) classifies the articulation of vowels according to three factors: height (vertical position of the tongue); backness (horizontal position of the tongue); and roundedness (shape of the lips). The different vowel sounds are shown in the diagram (above right), which can be viewed as a sideview of the human mouth, with the bottom-right corner being the lower-back and the top-left being the upper-front.

From this you can see that the 'a' sound in 'hat' (represented by 'a' in the IPA) is formed with the tongue low, away from the roof of the mouth at the front. The 'oo' sound in 'boot' (represented by 'u' in the IPA) is formed with the tongue close to the roof of the mouth at the back and

the lips rounded.

So what of y? We're taught that there are five vowels in the English alphabet, 'a', 'e', 'i', 'o' and 'u'. But in words like 'my' and 'mow', 'y' and 'w' act as vowels. However, both also act as consonants, in words like buying and mowing, although their pronunciation does not involve the complete block of airflow that defines a consonant. For this reason, 'w' and 'y' are known as semi-vowels.

Before we leave vowels, a couple of oddities. The words 'facetious' and 'abstemious' feature all five vowels in the correct order, while 'queueing' (which could also be spelt 'queuing', but that would spoil the trick!) contains five consecutive vowels.

See also ASSONANCE; DIPHTHONG; LIBRETTO; PHONETICS.

WEATHER

It has been said that the Inuit and other northern peoples have a hundred different words for snow. This is actually an exaggeration of an observation made by anthropologist Franz Boas that they have four different words for snow, whereas English has one, his point being that the way we live dictates the vocabulary that we develop.

In return, the northern peoples probably joke about the number of words in English for rain, wind and all the other forms of weather that dominate our daily lives.

PRECIPITATION	WIND
blizzard	*breeze*
cloudburst	*gale*
deluge	*gust*
downpour	*hurricane*
drizzle	*tornado*
flurry	*zephyr*
fog	
hail	

COMBINATIONS

mist	
rain	*squall*
shower	*storm*
sleet	*tempest*

WEBSTER, NOAH (1758–1843)

Described as 'the father of American scholarship and education', Noah Webster was the man who established American English through his writing of two groundbreaking publications: *A Grammatical Institute of the English Language* and *An American Dictionary of the English Language*.

The former was a three-part teaching aid consisting of a spelling book, a grammar book and a reading book. It was the spelling book that showed the first real signs of Webster's revolutionary attitude towards what he described as 'the clamor of pedantry' that had come to govern English grammar and spelling. The fashion amongst the English educated classes at the time was for peppering the language with Greek and Latin and inventing grammatical rules that had their basis in those ancient languages, for example the split infinitive. However, Webster set out to simplify spelling along more straightforward Anglo-Saxon lines and thus create a standard that would unify the way English was used across America.

Here are some of the typical spelling changes Webster made:

C TO S ⟹ offence ⟹ offense   NO U ⟹ favour ⟹ favor
OUGH TO OW ⟹ plough ⟹ plow   RE TO ER ⟹ centre ⟹ center
NO DOUBLE LETTERS ⟹ travelling ⟹ traveling

Webster's spelling book was a massive success. Known fondly as 'the blue-backed speller' because of its cover, it was used for over a hundred years as a standard textbook in American schools. It sold over 100 million copies and became a nice little earner for its author.

But it was not enough for Webster. In 1807 he embarked upon what would become a 20-year project, *An American Dictionary of the English Language*, during the course of which he learnt 26 languages and made study trips to Europe to help him beef up his definitions and etymologies. The resultant dictionary rivalled Samuel Johnson's for its thoroughness and authority. It contained 12,000 words that had never appeared in an English dictionary before, together with nearly 60,000 that had, albeit with different spellings in many cases.

Upon Webster's death in 1843 his dictionary legacy was bought by G. & C. Merriam & Co, who continued to update and publish what is now called the *Merriam-Webster Dictionary*. It is the second-biggest selling book in the English language after the Bible.

WHY

'Tidy your room.'
'Why?'
'Because I say so.'
'Why?'
'Because I'm tired of all this mess.'
'Why?'
'Because mess is stressful.'
'Why?'
'Because it upsets my sense of calm.'
'Why?'
'I've explained that.'
'Why?'
'Because you asked me to.'
'Why?'
'I don't know, you tell me.'
'Why?'
'You're really starting to irritate me.'
'Why?'

'Because you keep asking me why.'
'Why?'
'I wish I knew.'
'Why?'
'I don't really, it's just an expression.'
'Why?'

In the wrong hands, 'why' can be the most annoying word in the English language.

In its Old English form it was spelt with the 'h' before the 'w', and either an 'a', a 'y' or an 'i'. It was pronounced with an aspirate 'h', like a sigh before the 'w', as it still is in some dialects such as those in certain areas of Scotland.

WHILE OR WHILST?

Which is correct? The answer is both. Derived from the Old English 'hwil', they have been used interchangeably since the Middle Ages. Nevertheless, 'whilst' is generally held to be the more old-fashioned of the two, probably because that 'st' ending seems archaic.

As with all words, it is usage that keeps them alive and we have to surmise that it is the pleasure of saying such words that protects them from extinction. The 'st' enables one word to flow into the next more gently, as you'll notice if you compare these phrases:

> 'COME AMONGST US.' *'Come among us.'*
> 'AMIDST HIS FOLLOWERS.' *'Amid his followers.'*
> 'WHILST APPROACHING THE CITY.' *'While approaching the city.'*

Other words that are interchangeable in English are:

> ON ❖ UPON ❖ THOUGH ❖ ALTHOUGH ❖ TOWARD ❖ TOWARDS

'Again' and 'against', however, have quite different meanings today, although they stem from the same meaning of 'in the opposite direction'. Phrases like 'to and again' (to and fro) gave it a sense of returning to the beginning. Other phrases like 'they answered again' (answered back) evolved into a sense of repetition. Hence the modern meaning of again.

WORD

The innocent little word that prompted this entire book, 'word' is Germanic in origin and has been spelt the same way for over a thousand years.

Most words in the English language are nouns, about a quarter are adjectives describing those nouns, roughly a seventh are verbs telling us what those nouns get up to and the rest are adverbs, prepositions, conjunctions, etc.

In 1973 Thomas Finkenstaedt and Dieter Wolff wrote *Ordered Profusion*, in which they published a survey carried out on a sample of approximately 80,000 words in the *Shorter Oxford Dictionary*. Their aim had been to deduce what proportion of words in English had come from Latin, French, Greek, Germanic, etc. Their findings were as follows:

FRENCH, INCLUDING OLD FRENCH AND EARLY ANGLO-FRENCH: 28.3%

LATIN, INCLUDING MODERN SCIENTIFIC AND TECHNICAL LATIN: 28.24%

OLD AND MIDDLE ENGLISH, OLD NORSE, AND DUTCH: 25%

GREEK: 5.32%

NO ETYMOLOGY GIVEN: 4.03%

DERIVED FROM PROPER NAMES: 3.28%

ALL OTHER LANGUAGES CONTRIBUTED LESS THAN 1%

In spite of this highly developed vocabulary, some theorists claim that words actually get in the way of communication. 'Wordless' languages, they say, such as body language, music or art, communicate far more effectively with our inner emotions than straightforward, down-to-earth words. Whether that's true or not, words remain our primary mode of communication, whether written or spoken.

I give you my word ✳ *I'm lost for words* ✳ *Mark my words* ✳ *Mum's the word* ✳ *That's not the word* ✳ *The word on the street* ✳ *Too angry for words* ✳ *Word for word* ✳ *Word of mouth* ✳ *Word up* ✳ *Words cannot express* ✳ *Words fail me*

WORDS OF WISDOM

Without words, how would we pass on our wisdom? Without wisdom, how would we pass on our words? This is the classic structure to follow if you want to say something pithy that goes down in history. It also helps to have done something famous. A glance through the vast collections of famous words of wisdom shows very few attributed to unknowns.

ON WISDOM

'Wisdom is the reward you get for a lifetime of listening when you would rather have talked.'
Mark Twain

✳

'Silence does not always mark wisdom.'
Samuel Taylor Coleridge

✳

'Life is a festival only to the wise.'
Ralph Waldo Emerson

✳

'The more a man knows, the more he forgives.'
Catherine the Great

'A loving heart is the truest wisdom.'
Charles Dickens

✳

'The wisdom of nations lies in their proverbs, which are brief and pithy.'
William Penn

✳

'More than anytime in history mankind faces a crossroads. One path leads to despair and utter hopelessness, the other to total extinction. Let us pray that we have the wisdom to choose correctly.'
Woody Allen

ON BEHAVIOUR

'A tyrant is always stirring up some war or other, in order that the people may require a leader.'
Plato

'There are two ways of spreading light: to be the candle or the mirror that reflects it.'
Edith Wharton

'You can't cross a chasm in two small jumps.'
David Lloyd George

✳

'Am I not destroying my enemies when I make friends of them?'
Abraham Lincoln

✳

'We make a living by what we get. We make a life by what we give.'
Winston Churchill

✳

'Everything comes to him who hustles while he waits.' ·
Thomas A. Edison

✳

'No one can make you feel inferior without your consent.'
Eleanor Roosevelt

✳

'Everything should be made as simple as possible, but not simpler.'
Albert Einstein

✳

'But in this world nothing can be said to be certain, except death and taxes.'
Benjamin Franklin

✳

'If a man will begin with certainties, he shall end in doubts; but if he will be content to begin with doubts, he shall end in certainties.'
Francis Bacon

✳

'Nothing in life is to be feared. It is only to be understood.'
Marie Curie

✳

'It is impossible to enjoy idling thoroughly unless one has plenty of work to do.'
Jerome K. Jerome

✳

'Consistency is the last refuge of the unimaginative.'
Oscar Wilde

✳

'Trying is the first step toward failure.'
Homer Simpson

WRONG

Let us tell you WHAT'S WRONG The word 'wrong' has itself become a bit of a buzz word. 'That's just wrong,' is used about any sort of transgression, from a dodgy haircut to sexual deviancy (most commonly the latter).

Derived from the Old Norse *wrangr*, meaning unjust or awry, 'wrong' first came into English as a noun, which it still is, of course ('two wrongs don't make a right', etc.), as well as being an adjective, an adverb and a verb ('they have wronged us'). What we're looking at here, though, is the wrong use of words. For there are a number of words that are often used incorrectly out of ignorance of their true meaning – and that's not including the many instances of misquoted sayings (see Sayings).

♦ **disinterested** *commonly used as an alternative to uninterested since the 17th century, its proper meaning is, in fact, 'without a vested interest', or 'unprejudiced'.*

♦ **effect** *only a verb when meaning to bring about, as in 'to effect change'. Otherwise it is a noun, the verb being affect.*

♦ **enormity** *confused with enormous and assumed to be a noun formed from it, meaning hugeness, enormity actually means extreme wickedness.*

♦ **flounder** *a type of fish or the act of struggling violently for stability as if in quicksand. To break down or* sink like a ship is to founder.

♦ **of** *probably the most wrongly used word in English, 'of' is not part of the past conditional tense: 'I would of done it.' The word should be 'have'.*

♦ **pacific** *that's an ocean. If you mean something in particular, the word is specific.*

♦ **refute** *refute does not mean deny, the sense in which it is most commonly used – 'he refuted the allegations'. It means disprove.*

♦ **turgid** *often used about films or books to mean slow-moving or draggingly dull, the correct word is actually turbid. Turgid means swollen or puffed up.*

These wrongly used words, however, are but a snapshot in the history of the English language. It is often through the misuse of words that language evolves, new meanings are derived or new spellings develop. So what is wrong today may well be considered correct in a hundred years' time. What is important is that meaning does not become confused. The word 'disinterested' is an obvious example. It is so often used as a synonym for 'uninterested' that this is fast becoming its true meaning.

XMAS

There are shortened words and there are acronyms, but how many words feature a whole syllable reduced to a single letter that is not the initial of that letter? As shorthand for Christmas, Xmas has been with us for a couple of hundred years. Its formation is somewhat perplexing. You can understand why X might be a symbol for Christ, but then why is Christian never shortened to Xian, or christening to Xening? Because they look Chinese? Maybe. X is used as shorthand for 'cross' in, for example, King's X, but again this is not universal. As a warped extension of X representing the phonetic 'criss', Xtal has been used as engineers' slang for crystal for the last 50 years or so.

YES

Excuse me for getting a little bit personal, but what is the word you most frequently use at the height of sexual arousal? Is it 'cake'? 'chocolate'? 'champagne'?

I'll bet good money it's 'yes', whether that's a Meg Ryan 'YES! YES! YES!' or a more demur 'nyeeas'. Of all the good things in life that we could shout about when we're at our most ecstatic, the one word that leaps out every time is the simple affirmative.

> *When Hilary from Accounts agrees to go out with you – 'YES!'*
> *When you win the lottery – 'YES!'*
> *When your team scores a goal – 'YES!'*

The written-down word that we associated with exclamations of joy is 'hooray', but when was the last time you actually shouted 'hooray' spontaneously, or, for that matter, 'hurrah' or 'huzza', its etymological forerunners?

No, hooray is just an onomatopoeic attempt to capture the sound a cheering crowd makes in one word. You listen, next time you're in a cheering crowd. Nobody says hooray, they'll all be saying 'yes'.

ZYGOTE

This is where most English speakers' vocabularies stop. Schoolchildren tend to remember the words associated with reproduction, taught in biology lessons, and *zygote*, derived from a Greek word meaning 'yoked', is one of the most memorable of all, being the cell formed by the fertilization of the egg by the sperm. Although often cited as the last word in the dictionary, and indeed it is in some cases, at the time of writing 'zygote' sat 20 words in from the end of the *OED*.

ZYTHUM (THE LAST WORD)

A drink to end with then: zythum, in case you never bought a round in ancient Egypt, was a malt beer enjoyed by pyramid builders. More interesting still, it is currently the last word in *The Oxford English Dictionary*.

But the truly ingenious thing about zythum is that it's one of the few words you can still say after 15 pints of zythum.

List of books and websites used in the research of this book

American Heritage Dictionary, The, ed. Joe Pickett (Houghton Mifflin)

Brewer's Dictionary of Phrase and Fable, 15th edition (Cassell)

Burchfield, Robert, *The English Language* (Oxford University Press USA)

Cassell's Dictionary Of Slang, ed. Jonathon Green

Chambers Dictionary of Etymology, ed. Robert K. Barnhart

Cook, Vivian, *Accomodating Brocolli In The Cemetary* (Profile)

Crystal, David, *Words Words Words* (Oxford University Press)

Fowler, Henry, *Modern English Usage* (University Tutorial Press)

Hotten, John Camden, *The Slang Dictionary; Or, The Vulgar Words, Street Phrases, And Fast Expressions Of High And Low Society. Many With Their Etymology, And A Few With Their History Traced* (Elibron Classics)

Liberman, Anatoly, *Word Origins and How We Know Them* (Oxford University Press USA)

McQuain, Jeffrey, Malless, Stanley, *Coined by Shakespeare* (Merriam-Webster)

Oxford Reference Dictionary, The (Oxford University Press)

Stevenson, Victor, *The World of Words - An Illustrated History of Western Languages* (Sterling)

Wakelin, Martyn, *The Archaeology of English* (Batsford)

Wells, J.C., *Longman Pronunciation Dictionary* (Longman Education)

http://www.askoxford.com
http://www.behindthename.com
http://www.ethnologue.com
http://www.etymonline.com
http://www.hw-consultants.co.uk/hintonfamily/famous_quotes.htm
http://www.oed.com (Oxford English Dictionary Online)
http://www.universalteacher.org.uk
http://www.wikipedia.org
http://www.worldwidewords.org/turnsofphrase/tp-sho2.htm